To
Father Michael
with much appreciation
Timothy R. Botts
1997

# THE BOOK OF

# PSALMS

illustrated in expressive calligraphy by

*Timothy R. Botts*

Tyndale House Publishers, Inc.
WHEATON, ILLINOIS

Visit Tyndale's exciting Web site at www.tyndale.com

© 1997 by Timothy R. Botts. All rights reserved.

Page v is from a woodcut by Andy Botts.
Page 9 illustration of a man is by Jeremy Botts.

Pages 87, 133, and 141 are collaborations with Charles and
Gretchen Peterson, who did the marbling.

Published in association with the literary agency of Alive
Communications, Inc., 1465 Kelly Johnson Blvd., Suite 320,
Colorado Springs, CO 80920.

Scripture quotations are taken from the *Holy Bible,* New Living
Translation, copyright © 1996. Used by permission of Tyndale
House Publishers, Inc., Wheaton, Illinois 60189. All rights
reserved.

Library of Congress Cataloging-in-Publication Data

Bible. O.T. Psalms. English. New Living Translation. 1997.
    The book of Psalms / illustrated in expressive calligraphy
by Timothy R. Botts.
        p.    cm.
    ISBN 0-8423-4955-3 (hardcover : alk. paper)
    I. Botts, Timothy R.    II. Title.
BS1422 1997b
223'.20520834—dc21                                    97-10899

Printed in United States of America

03  02  01  00  99  98  97
7   6   5   4   3   2   1

*To Katy and Andrew*
*in celebration of your marriage*

PSALMS HAS BEEN CALLED THE HEART OF THE BIBLE both because of its central location and because of the full range of human emotions expressed here. We also get a broad view of God's greatness, as both glorious Ruler of the universe and intimately caring Father.

The Psalms are a treasure chest of metaphors, which artists love to work with. Included is visual imagery from ancient Hebrew culture as well as from more contemporary visual associations. You will find the flourishing tree of character, sheltering feathers, the pomegranate of fruitfulness, the harmonious flight of birds, tree rings portraying God's faithfulness to successive generations, and crashing cymbals.

I have added notes with each calligraphic piece to give you insight into the inspiration, my creative process, and the personal impact of the words. The references at the beginning of each note will help you find the verses in the Bible text. Sometimes only parts of verses are illustrated for the sake of simplicity or unity of the idea being expressed.

Having a melancholy temperament, I identify with the psalmist's ups and downs and draw strength from the unchanging promises of God within this book.

> *Give thanks to the LORD, for he is good!*
> *His faithful love endures forever.* Psalm 136:1

In Hebrew, *worship* means to bow down, reminding us that we should praise God with our whole being, not just with our mind. I hope your eyes and heart will be ignited in worship through this offering.

Let the song begin!

OH, THE JOYS OF THOSE
WHO DO NOT FOLLOW
OR STAND AROUND WITH SINNERS
BUT THEY DELIGHT IN DOING
DAY AND NIGHT
THEY ARE LIKE TREES
BEARING FRUIT EACH SEASON
THEIR LEAVES NEVER WITHER
AND IN ALL THEY DO.
THEY PROSPER
THEY PROSPER
THEY PROSPER

THE ADVICE OF THE WICKED
OR JOIN IN WITH SCOFFERS
EVERYTHING THE LORD WANTS
THEY THINK ABOUT HIS LAW
PLANTED ALONG THE RIVERBANK
WITHOUT FAIL

BOOK ONE (Psalms 1–41)

## PSALM 1

1 Oh, the joys of those
  who do not follow the advice of the wicked,
  or stand around with sinners,
  or join in with scoffers.
2 But they delight in doing everything the LORD
    wants;
  day and night they think about his law.
3 They are like trees planted along the riverbank,
  bearing fruit each season without fail.
  Their leaves never wither,
    and in all they do, they prosper.

4 But this is not true of the wicked.
  They are like worthless chaff, scattered by the
    wind.

PSALM 1:1-3  A tree is the perfect picture of the success we all desire. As we take in the nourishment of God's words, we can count on fruit to follow. This is the purpose I long for in my work. As an artist, I am in a better position to receive inspiration if I stay close to the one who inspires. In addition, these times of meditation are an antidote to cynicism.

5 They will be condemned at the time of
    judgment.
  Sinners will have no place among the godly.

6 For the LORD watches over the path of the
    godly,
  but the path of the wicked leads to
    destruction.

## PSALM 2

1 Why do the nations rage?
  Why do the people waste their time with
    futile plans?
2 The kings of the earth prepare for battle;
  the rulers plot together
 against the LORD
  and against his anointed one.
3 "Let us break their chains," they cry,
  "and free ourselves from this slavery."

4 But the one who rules in heaven laughs.
  The Lord scoffs at them.
5 Then in anger he rebukes them,
  terrifying them with his fierce fury.

⁶For the LORD declares, "I have placed my
    chosen king on the throne
    in Jerusalem, my holy city.*"

⁷The king proclaims the LORD's decree:
"The LORD said to me, `You are my son.*
    Today I have become your Father.*
⁸Only ask, and I will give you the nations as
        your inheritance,
    the ends of the earth as your possession.
⁹You will break them with an iron rod
    and smash them like clay pots.'"

¹⁰Now then, you kings, act wisely!
    Be warned, you rulers of the earth!
¹¹Serve the LORD with reverent fear,
    and rejoice with trembling.
¹²Submit to God's royal son, or he will become
        angry,
    and you will be destroyed in the midst of
        your pursuits—
    for his anger can flare up in an instant.

    But what joy for all who find protection in him!

## PSALM 3

*A psalm of David, regarding the time David fled from his son Absalom.*

¹O LORD, I have so many enemies;
    so many are against me.
²So many are saying,
    "God will never rescue him!"    *Interlude**

³But you, O LORD, are a shield around me,
    my glory, and the one who lifts my head high.
⁴I cried out to the LORD,
    and he answered me from his holy mountain.
        *Interlude*

⁵I lay down and slept.
    I woke up in safety,
    for the LORD was watching over me.
⁶I am not afraid of ten thousand enemies
    who surround me on every side.

⁷Arise, O LORD!
    Rescue me, my God!

Slap all my enemies in the face!
    Shatter the teeth of the wicked!

⁸Victory comes from you, O LORD.
    May your blessings rest on your people.
        *Interlude*

## PSALM 4

*For the choir director: A psalm of David, to be accompanied by stringed instruments.*

¹Answer me when I call,
    O God who declares me innocent.
    Take away my distress.
    Have mercy on me and hear my prayer.

²How long will you people ruin my reputation?
    How long will you make these groundless
        accusations?
    How long will you pursue lies?    *Interlude*

³You can be sure of this:
    The LORD has set apart the godly for himself.
    The LORD will answer when I call to him.

⁴Don't sin by letting anger gain control over you.
    Think about it overnight and remain silent.
        *Interlude*
⁵Offer proper sacrifices,
    and trust in the LORD.

⁶Many people say, "Who will show us better
        times?"
    Let the smile of your face shine on us,
    LORD.
⁷You have given me greater joy
    than those who have abundant harvests
        of grain and wine.

⁸I will lie down in peace and sleep,
    for you alone, O LORD, will keep me safe.

PSALM 2:1-4  Do we really think we can outwit God? This composition illustrates the contrast between the complex but petty mess of human conflict and the incredible dimensions of the Almighty's reply. Artists often strengthen their work when they change their perspective. By considering the world's raging from God's point of view, I was able to create a more dramatic design of surprising proportions.

2:6 Hebrew *on Zion, my holy mountain.*  2:7a Or *Son;* also in 2:12.  2:7b Or *Today I reveal you as my son.*  3:2 Hebrew *Selah.* The meaning of this word is uncertain, though it is probably a musical or literary term. It is rendered *Interlude* throughout the Psalms.

But the one who rules in heaven laughs.
The one who rules in heaven laughs.

Why
do the nations
rage?
Why do the people
waste their time
with futile plans?

The kings of the earth
prepare for battle;
The rulers plot together
against the LORD
and against his anointed one.
"Let us break their chains," they cry,
"and free ourselves
from this slavery."

# PSALM 5

*For the choir director: A psalm of David, to be accompanied by the flute.*

¹O LORD, hear me as I pray;
pay attention to my groaning.
²Listen to my cry for help, my King and my God,
for I will never pray to anyone but you.
³Listen to my voice in the morning, LORD.
Each morning I bring my requests to you and wait expectantly.

⁴O God, you take no pleasure in wickedness;
you cannot tolerate the slightest sin.
⁵Therefore, the proud will not be allowed to stand in your presence,
for you hate all who do evil.
⁶You will destroy those who tell lies.
The LORD detests murderers and deceivers.

⁷Because of your unfailing love, I can enter your house;
with deepest awe I will worship at your Temple.
⁸Lead me in the right path, O LORD,
or my enemies will conquer me.
Tell me clearly what to do,
and show me which way to turn.

⁹My enemies cannot speak one truthful word.
Their deepest desire is to destroy others.
Their talk is foul, like the stench from an open grave.
Their speech is filled with flattery.
¹⁰O God, declare them guilty.
Let them be caught in their own traps.
Drive them away because of their many sins,
for they rebel against you.
¹¹But let all who take refuge in you rejoice;
let them sing joyful praises forever.
Protect them,
so all who love your name may be filled with joy.
¹²For you bless the godly, O LORD,
surrounding them with your shield of love.

# PSALM 6

*For the choir director: A psalm of David, to be accompanied by an eight-stringed instrument.***

¹O LORD, do not rebuke me in your anger
or discipline me in your rage.
²Have compassion on me, LORD, for I am weak.
Heal me, LORD, for my body is in agony.
³I am sick at heart.
How long, O LORD, until you restore me?

⁴Return, O LORD, and rescue me.
Save me because of your unfailing love.
⁵For in death, who remembers you?
Who can praise you from the grave?

⁶I am worn out from sobbing.
Every night tears drench my bed;
my pillow is wet from weeping.
⁷My vision is blurred by grief;
my eyes are worn out because of all my enemies.

⁸Go away, all you who do evil,
for the LORD has heard my crying.
⁹The LORD has heard my plea;
the LORD will answer my prayer.
¹⁰May all my enemies be disgraced and terrified.
May they suddenly turn back in shame.

# PSALM 7

*A psalm of David, which he sang to the LORD concerning Cush of the tribe of Benjamin.*

¹I come to you for protection, O LORD my God.
Save me from my persecutors—rescue me!
²If you don't, they will maul me like a lion,
tearing me to pieces with no one to rescue me.

³O LORD my God, if I have done wrong
or am guilty of injustice,
⁴if I have betrayed a friend
or plundered my enemy without cause,
⁵then let my enemies capture me.
Let them trample me into the ground.
Let my honor be left in the dust.          *Interlude*

6:TITLE Hebrew *with stringed instruments; according to the sheminith.*

6 Arise, O LORD, in anger!
  Stand up against the fury of my enemies!
  Wake up, my God, and bring justice!
7 Gather the nations before you.
  Sit on your throne high above them.
8 The LORD passes judgment on the nations.
  Declare me righteous, O LORD,
    for I am innocent, O Most High!
9 End the wickedness of the ungodly,
  but help all those who obey you.
  For you look deep within the mind and heart,
    O righteous God.

10 God is my shield,
  saving those whose hearts are true and right.
11 God is a judge who is perfectly fair.
  He is angry with the wicked every day.

12 If a person does not repent,
  God* will sharpen his sword;
  he will bend and string his bow.
13 He will prepare his deadly weapons
  and ignite his flaming arrows.

14 The wicked conceive evil;
  they are pregnant with trouble
  and give birth to lies.
15 They dig a pit to trap others
  and then fall into it themselves.
16 They make trouble,
  but it backfires on them.
  They plan violence for others,
  but it falls on their own heads.

17 I will thank the LORD because he is just;
  I will sing praise to the name of the LORD
    Most High.

## PSALM 8

*For the choir director: A psalm of David, to be accompanied by a stringed instrument.*

1 O LORD, our Lord, the majesty of your name
    fills the earth!
  Your glory is higher than the heavens.

2 You have taught children and nursing infants
    to give you praise.*

O GOD
YOU TAKE
NO PLEASURE
IN WICKEDNESS
YOU CANNOT TOLERATE
THE SLIGHTEST SIN

THEREFORE
The proud will not be allowed
to stand in your presence
for you hate all who do evil

PSALM 5:4-5   Sometimes God is described as totally "other" to explain how different his character is from our own. My goal was to picture our separation from God caused by our pride. This challenged my artistic mind to think oppositely: purity versus deceit and order versus confusion.

They silence your enemies
  who were seeking revenge.

3 When I look at the night sky and see the work
    of your fingers—
  the moon and the stars you have set in
    place—

7:12 Hebrew *he.* 8:TITLE Hebrew *according to the gittith.* 8:2 As in Greek version; Hebrew reads *to show strength.*

5

⁴what are mortals that you should think
      of us,
    mere humans that you should care for us?*
⁵For you made us only a little lower than God,*
    and you crowned us with glory and honor.
⁶You put us in charge of everything you made,
    giving us authority over all things—
⁷the sheep and the cattle
    and all the wild animals,
⁸the birds in the sky, the fish in the sea,
    and everything that swims the ocean
      currents.

⁹O LORD, our Lord, the majesty of your name
    fills the earth!

## PSALM 9

*For the choir director: A psalm of David, to be sung
to the tune "Death of the Son."*

¹I will thank you, LORD, with all my heart;
    I will tell of all the marvelous things you
      have done.
²I will be filled with joy because of you.
    I will sing praises to your name, O Most
      High.

³My enemies turn away in retreat;
    they are overthrown and destroyed before
      you.
⁴For you have judged in my favor;
    from your throne, you have judged with
      fairness.

⁵You have rebuked the nations and destroyed
      the wicked;
    you have wiped out their names forever.
⁶My enemies have met their doom;
    their cities are perpetual ruins.
    Even the memory of their uprooted cities
      is lost.

⁷But the LORD reigns forever,
    executing judgment from his throne.
⁸He will judge the world with justice
    and rule the nations with fairness.

⁹The LORD is a shelter for the oppressed,
    a refuge in times of trouble.
¹⁰Those who know your name trust in you,
    for you, O LORD, have never abandoned
      anyone who searches for you.

¹¹Sing praises to the LORD who reigns in
      Jerusalem.*
    Tell the world about his unforgettable deeds.
¹²For he who avenges murder cares for the
      helpless.
    He does not ignore those who cry to him
      for help.

¹³LORD, have mercy on me.
    See how I suffer at the hands of those who
      hate me.
    Snatch me back from the jaws of death.
¹⁴Save me, so I can praise you publicly at
      Jerusalem's gates,
    so I can rejoice that you have rescued me.

¹⁵The nations have fallen into the pit they dug
      for others.
    They have been caught in their own trap.
¹⁶The LORD is known for his justice.
    The wicked have trapped themselves in their
      own snares.    *Quiet Interlude**

¹⁷The wicked will go down to the grave.*
    This is the fate of all the nations who ignore
      God.
¹⁸For the needy will not be forgotten
      forever;
    the hopes of the poor will not always be
      crushed.

¹⁹Arise, O LORD!
    Do not let mere mortals defy you!
    Let the nations be judged in your presence!

PSALM 6:2-3, 6, 9  When our health fails, our
mental outlook is affected. This is illustrated by the
indistinct writing in the background. The psalmist's confidence in the Lord is contrasted with the more solid
words in white. This piece is an example of where
the process—such as dripping the paint—causes me
to actively enter into the meaning of the words.

**8:4** Hebrew *what is man that you should think of him, the son of man that you should care for him?*  **8:5** Or *a little lower than the angels;* Hebrew reads *Elohim.*  **9:11** Hebrew
*Zion;* also in 9:14.  **9:16** Hebrew *Higgaion Selah.* The meaning of this phrase is uncertain.  **9:17** Hebrew *to Sheol.*

Have
compassion
on me, LORD,
for I am weak.
Heal me, LORD,
for my body is in agony.

I am sick at heart.

THE LORD HAS HEARD MY PLEA

How long, O LORD

THE LORD WILL ANSWER MY PRAYER

until you restore me?

I am worn out
from sobbing.
Every night tears drench my bed;
my pillow is wet from weeping.

20 Make them tremble in fear, O LORD.
   Let them know they are merely human.
      *Interlude*

## PSALM 10

1 O LORD, why do you stand so far away?
   Why do you hide when I need you the most?
2 Proud and wicked people viciously oppress the
      poor.
   Let them be caught in the evil they plan for
      others.
3 For they brag about their evil desires;
   they praise the greedy and curse the LORD.
4 These wicked people are too proud to seek God.
   They seem to think that God is dead.
5 Yet they succeed in everything they do.
   They do not see your punishment awaiting
      them.
   They pour scorn on all their enemies.
6 They say to themselves, "Nothing bad will ever
      happen to us!
   We will be free of trouble forever!"

7 Their mouths are full of cursing, lies, and
      threats.
   Trouble and evil are on the tips of their
      tongues.
8 They lurk in dark alleys,
   murdering the innocent who pass by.

   They are always searching
      for some helpless victim.
9 Like lions they crouch silently,
      waiting to pounce on the helpless.
   Like hunters they capture their victims
      and drag them away in nets.
10 The helpless are overwhelmed and collapse;
   they fall beneath the strength of the wicked.
11 The wicked say to themselves, "God isn't
      watching!
   He will never notice!"

12 Arise, O LORD!
   Punish the wicked, O God!
   Do not forget the helpless!
13 Why do the wicked get away with cursing God?
   How can they think, "God will never call us
      to account"?

14 But you do see the trouble and grief they
      cause.
   You take note of it and punish them.
   The helpless put their trust in you.
   You are the defender of orphans.

15 Break the arms of these wicked, evil people!
   Go after them until the last one is
      destroyed!
16 The LORD is king forever and ever!
   Let those who worship other gods be swept
      from the land.

17 LORD, you know the hopes of the helpless.
   Surely you will listen to their cries and
      comfort them.
18 You will bring justice to the orphans and the
      oppressed,
   so people can no longer terrify them.

## PSALM 11

*For the choir director: A psalm of David.*

1 I trust in the LORD for protection.
   So why do you say to me,
 "Fly to the mountains for safety!
2    The wicked are stringing their bows
      and setting their arrows in the bowstrings.
   They shoot from the shadows at those who
      do right.
3 The foundations of law and order have
      collapsed.
   What can the righteous do?"

4 But the LORD is in his holy Temple;
   the LORD still rules from heaven.
   He watches everything closely,
      examining everyone on earth.
5 The LORD examines both the righteous and
      the wicked.
   He hates everyone who loves violence.

PSALM 8:3-9  Maps of the constellations intrigue
me. People have been able to recognize these same
celestial patterns throughout the centuries even though
the stars and the earth are all moving! Here I tried to
show our position in the created order. We are subject
to the Master of the universe, but he has given us
enormous power and potential. What a magnificent
relationship is ours!

# O LORD OUR LORD

When I look at the night sky and see the work of your fingers
the moon and the stars you have set in place
What are mortals that you should think of us,
mere humans that you should care for us?
For you made us only a little lower than God
and you crowned us with glory and honor
you put us in charge of everything you made
giving us authority over all things

# THE MAJESTY OF
# YOUR NAME

the sheep and the cattle
and all the wild animals
the birds in the sky
the fish in the sea
and everything that swims
the ocean currents

# FILLS THE EARTH

⁶He rains down blazing coals on the wicked,
  punishing them with burning sulfur and
    scorching winds.
⁷For the LORD is righteous, and he loves justice.
  Those who do what is right will see his face.

## PSALM 12

*For the choir director: A psalm of David, to be accompanied by an eight-stringed instrument.*\*

¹Help, O LORD, for the godly are fast
    disappearing!
  The faithful have vanished from the earth!
²Neighbors lie to each other,
  speaking with flattering lips and insincere
    hearts.
³May the LORD bring their flattery to an
    end
  and silence their proud tongues.
⁴They say, "We will lie to our hearts' content.
  Our lips are our own—who can stop us?"

⁵The LORD replies, "I have seen violence
    done to the helpless,
  and I have heard the groans of the poor.
  Now I will rise up to rescue them,
    as they have longed for me to do."
⁶The LORD's promises are pure,
  like silver refined in a furnace,
    purified seven times over.

⁷Therefore, LORD, we know you will protect
    the oppressed,
  preserving them forever from this lying
    generation,
⁸even though the wicked strut about,
  and evil is praised throughout the land.

## PSALM 13

*For the choir director: A psalm of David.*

¹O LORD, how long will you forget me?
    Forever?
  How long will you look the other way?
²How long must I struggle with anguish in my
    soul,
  with sorrow in my heart every day?

How long will my enemy have the upper
    hand?
³Turn and answer me, O LORD my God!
  Restore the light to my eyes, or I will die.
⁴Don't let my enemies gloat, saying, "We have
    defeated him!"
  Don't let them rejoice at my downfall.

⁵But I trust in your unfailing love.
  I will rejoice because you have rescued me.
⁶I will sing to the LORD
  because he has been so good to me.

## PSALM 14

*For the choir director: A psalm of David.*

¹Only fools say in their hearts,
    "There is no God."
  They are corrupt, and their actions are evil;
    no one does good!

²The LORD looks down from heaven
  on the entire human race;
  he looks to see if there is even one with real
    understanding,
    one who seeks for God.
³But no, all have turned away from God;
  all have become corrupt.
  No one does good,
    not even one!

⁴Will those who do evil never learn?
  They eat up my people like bread;
    they wouldn't think of praying to the LORD.
⁵Terror will grip them,
  for God is with those who obey him.
⁶The wicked frustrate the plans of the
    oppressed,
  but the LORD will protect his people.

✎ PSALM 11:3-4, 7  The Ten Commandments have been the moral basis for our culture for centuries. So when these absolutes are ignored, we wonder if our civilization can be saved. The key issue is this: Does it matter how I live? When I brainstorm a design, I try to draw parallels from a text. In this case the imagery of sight is repeated and gives us the answer: Yes, because God sees us, and someday we will see him!

**12:**TITLE Hebrew *according to the sheminith.*

BUT THE LORD IS

IN HIS HOLY TEMPLE

THE LORD STILL RULES FROM HEAVEN

HE WATCHES EVERYTHING CLOSELY

EXAMINING EVERYONE ON EARTH

For the LORD is righteous, and he loves justice
those who do what is right will see his face

THE
FOUNDATIONS
OF LAW
AND ORDER
HAVE COLLAPSED
WHAT CAN THE
RIGHTEOUS
DO?

7 Oh, that salvation would come from Mount
   Zion to rescue Israel!
   For when the LORD restores his people,
   Jacob will shout with joy, and Israel will
   rejoice.

## PSALM 15

*A psalm of David.*

1 Who may worship in your sanctuary, LORD?
   Who may enter your presence on your holy
   hill?

2 Those who lead blameless lives
   and do what is right,
   speaking the truth from sincere hearts.
3 Those who refuse to slander others
   or harm their neighbors
   or speak evil of their friends.
4 Those who despise persistent sinners,
   and honor the faithful followers of the LORD
   and keep their promises even when it hurts.
5 Those who do not charge interest on the
   money they lend,
   and who refuse to accept bribes to testify
   against the innocent.

Such people will stand firm forever.

## PSALM 16

*A psalm of David.*

1 Keep me safe, O God,
   for I have come to you for refuge.

2 I said to the LORD, "You are my Master!
   All the good things I have are from you."
3 The godly people in the land
   are my true heroes!
   I take pleasure in them!
4 Those who chase after other gods will be filled
   with sorrow.
   I will not take part in their sacrifices
   or even speak the names of their gods.

5 LORD, you alone are my inheritance, my cup
   of blessing.
   You guard all that is mine.

6 The land you have given me is a pleasant
   land.
   What a wonderful inheritance!

7 I will bless the LORD who guides me;
   even at night my heart instructs me.
8 I know the LORD is always with me.
   I will not be shaken, for he is right beside me.

9 No wonder my heart is filled with joy,
   and my mouth* shouts his praises!
   My body rests in safety.
10 For you will not leave my soul among the
   dead*
   or allow your godly one* to rot in the grave.
11 You will show me the way of life,
   granting me the joy of your presence
   and the pleasures of living with you forever.

## PSALM 17

*A prayer of David.*

1 O LORD, hear my plea for justice.
   Listen to my cry for help.
   Pay attention to my prayer,
   for it comes from an honest heart.
2 Declare me innocent,
   for you know those who do right.

3 You have tested my thoughts and examined my
   heart in the night.
   You have scrutinized me and found nothing
   amiss,
   for I am determined not to sin in what I say.
4 I have followed your commands,
   which have kept me from going along with
   cruel and evil people.
5 My steps have stayed on your path;
   I have not wavered from following you.

✒ PSALM 15:1-5  Sometimes we may ask what
difference it makes if we have good character. These
verses show that there is a payoff. In a longer text such
as this, I often find a key phrase that summarizes the
various parts. In this case it becomes a hook, which
causes you to read further to find out who *will* stand
firm. The background symbolizes that people of such
integrity are the real stars among us.

16:9 As in Greek version; Hebrew reads *glory.*  16:10a Hebrew *in Sheol.*  16:10b Or *your Holy One.*

THOSE WHO LEAD
BLAMELESS LIVES
AND DO WHAT IS RIGHT
speaking the truth
from sincere hearts

Those who refuse
to slander others
or harm their neighbors
or speak evil of their friends
Those who despise persistent sinners
AND
honor the faithful followers of the Lord
AND KEEP
THEIR PROMISES
EVEN WHEN
IT HURTS

Those who do not charge interest
on the money they l e n d
and who refuse to accept bribes
to testify
against the i n n o c e n t

such people will stand firm forever

⁶I am praying to you because I know you will
  answer, O God.
    Bend down and listen as I pray.
⁷Show me your unfailing love in wonderful
  ways.
    You save with your strength
    those who seek refuge from their enemies.
⁸Guard me as the apple of your eye.
    Hide me in the shadow of your wings.
⁹Protect me from wicked people who attack me,
    from murderous enemies who surround me.

¹⁰They are without pity.
    Listen to their boasting.
¹¹They track me down, surround me,
    and throw me to the ground.
¹²They are like hungry lions, eager to tear me
  apart—
    like young lions in hiding, waiting for their
    chance.

¹³Arise, O LORD!
    Stand against them and bring them to their
    knees!
    Rescue me from the wicked with your
    sword!
¹⁴Save me by your mighty hand, O LORD,
    from those whose only concern is earthly
    gain.
  May they have their punishment in full.
    May their children inherit more of the same,
    and may the judgment continue to their
    children's children.

¹⁵But because I have done what is right, I will
  see you.
    When I awake, I will be fully satisfied,
    for I will see you face to face.

## PSALM 18

*For the choir director: A psalm of David, the servant of the*
*LORD. He sang this song to the LORD on the day the*
*LORD rescued him from all his enemies and from Saul.*

¹I love you, LORD; you are my strength.
²The LORD is my rock, my fortress, and my
  savior;

my God is my rock, in whom I find
  protection.
    He is my shield, the strength of my salvation,
    and my stronghold.
³I will call on the LORD, who is worthy
  of praise,
    for he saves me from my enemies.

⁴The ropes of death surrounded me;
    the floods of destruction swept over me.
⁵The grave* wrapped its ropes around me;
    death itself stared me in the face.
⁶But in my distress I cried out to the LORD;
    yes, I prayed to my God for help.
  He heard me from his sanctuary;
    my cry reached his ears.

⁷Then the earth quaked and trembled;
    the foundations of the mountains shook;
    they quaked because of his anger.
⁸Smoke poured from his nostrils;
    fierce flames leaped from his mouth;
    glowing coals flamed forth from him.
⁹He opened the heavens and came down;
    dark storm clouds were beneath his feet.
¹⁰Mounted on a mighty angel,* he flew,
    soaring on the wings of the wind.
¹¹He shrouded himself in darkness,
    veiling his approach with dense rain
    clouds.
¹²The brilliance of his presence broke through
    the clouds,
    raining down hail and burning coals.
¹³The LORD thundered from heaven;
    the Most High gave a mighty shout.*
¹⁴He shot his arrows and scattered his enemies;
    his lightning flashed, and they were greatly
    confused.
¹⁵Then at your command, O LORD,
    at the blast of your breath,
  the bottom of the sea could be seen,
    and the foundations of the earth were laid
    bare.

¹⁶He reached down from heaven and rescued
  me;
    he drew me out of deep waters.

---

18:5 Hebrew *Sheol.*  18:10 Hebrew *a cherub.*  18:13 As in Greek version (see also 2 Sam 22:14); Hebrew adds *raining down hail and burning coals.*

<sup>17</sup> He delivered me from my powerful enemies,
from those who hated me and were too
strong for me.
<sup>18</sup> They attacked me at a moment when I was
weakest,
but the LORD upheld me.
<sup>19</sup> He led me to a place of safety;
he rescued me because he delights in me.
<sup>20</sup> The LORD rewarded me for doing right;
he compensated me because of my
innocence.
<sup>21</sup> For I have kept the ways of the LORD;
I have not turned from my God to follow
evil.
<sup>22</sup> For all his laws are constantly before me;
I have never abandoned his principles.
<sup>23</sup> I am blameless before God;
I have kept myself from sin.
<sup>24</sup> The LORD rewarded me for doing right,
because of the innocence of my hands in his
sight.

<sup>25</sup> To the faithful you show yourself faithful;
to those with integrity you show integrity.
<sup>26</sup> To the pure you show yourself pure,
but to the wicked you show yourself
hostile.
<sup>27</sup> You rescue those who are humble,
but you humiliate the proud.
<sup>28</sup> LORD, you have brought light to my life;
my God, you light up my darkness.
<sup>29</sup> In your strength I can crush an army;
with my God I can scale any wall.

<sup>30</sup> As for God, his way is perfect.
All the LORD's promises prove true.
He is a shield for all who look to him for
protection.
<sup>31</sup> For who is God except the LORD?
Who but our God is a solid rock?
<sup>32</sup> God arms me with strength;
he has made my way safe.
<sup>33</sup> He makes me as surefooted as a deer,
leading me safely along the mountain
heights.
<sup>34</sup> He prepares me for battle;
he strengthens me to draw a bow of bronze.

PSALM 17:8 The poetic richness of Psalms is particularly evident in the double metaphor in this single verse. It reminds me of my relationship to Arnold Bank, who taught me so much about calligraphy. He was a stern man who rarely complimented me, but I knew that he cared for me by the occasional twinkle in his eye. If you slice an apple crosswise, you get this star pattern.

<sup>35</sup> You have given me the shield of your
salvation.
Your right hand supports me;
your gentleness has made me great.
<sup>36</sup> You have made a wide path for my feet
to keep them from slipping.

<sup>37</sup> I chased my enemies and caught them;
I did not stop until they were conquered.

<sup>38</sup>I struck them down so they could not get up;
they fell beneath my feet.
<sup>39</sup>You have armed me with strength for the
battle;
you have subdued my enemies under my
feet.
<sup>40</sup>You made them turn and run;
I have destroyed all who hated me.
<sup>41</sup>They called for help, but no one came to
rescue them.
They cried to the LORD, but he refused to
answer them.
<sup>42</sup>I ground them as fine as dust carried by the
wind.
I swept them into the gutter like dirt.

<sup>43</sup>You gave me victory over my accusers.
You appointed me as the ruler over nations;
people I don't even know now serve me.
<sup>44</sup>As soon as they hear of me, they submit;
foreigners cringe before me.
<sup>45</sup>They all lose their courage
and come trembling from their strongholds.

<sup>46</sup>The LORD lives! Blessed be my rock!
May the God of my salvation be exalted!
<sup>47</sup>He is the God who pays back those who harm
me;
he subdues the nations under me
<sup>48</sup> and rescues me from my enemies.
You hold me safe beyond the reach of my
enemies;
you save me from violent opponents.
<sup>49</sup>For this, O LORD, I will praise you among the
nations;
I will sing joyfully to your name.
<sup>50</sup>You give great victories to your king;
you show unfailing love to your anointed,
to David and all his descendants forever.

## PSALM 19

*For the choir director: A psalm of David.*

<sup>1</sup>The heavens tell of the glory of God.
The skies display his marvelous
craftsmanship.

<sup>2</sup>Day after day they continue to speak;
night after night they make him known.
<sup>3</sup>They speak without a sound or a word;
their voice is silent in the skies;*
<sup>4</sup>yet their message has gone out to all the earth,
and their words to all the world.

The sun lives in the heavens
where God placed it.
<sup>5</sup>It bursts forth like a radiant bridegroom
after his wedding.
It rejoices like a great athlete
eager to run the race.
<sup>6</sup>The sun rises at one end of the heavens
and follows its course to the other end.
Nothing can hide from its heat.

<sup>7</sup>The law of the LORD is perfect,
reviving the soul.
The decrees of the LORD are trustworthy,
making wise the simple.
<sup>8</sup>The commandments of the LORD are right,
bringing joy to the heart.
The commands of the LORD are clear,
giving insight to life.
<sup>9</sup>Reverence for the LORD is pure,
lasting forever.
The laws of the LORD are true;
each one is fair.
<sup>10</sup>They are more desirable than gold,
even the finest gold.
They are sweeter than honey,
even honey dripping from the comb.
<sup>11</sup>They are a warning to those who hear them;
there is great reward for those who obey them.

<sup>12</sup>How can I know all the sins lurking in my
heart?
Cleanse me from these hidden faults.

PSALM 18:16-19   After some of the darker psalms that leave us hanging, this one shifts to a testimony of God's saving action. Some of my favorite childhood memories are of annual vacations to the seashore. I never remember being afraid of the ocean because my father, who was much stronger than I, held me up against the force of the waves. This is the basis for the large gesture in the background.

**19:3** Or *There is no speech or language where their voice is not heard.*

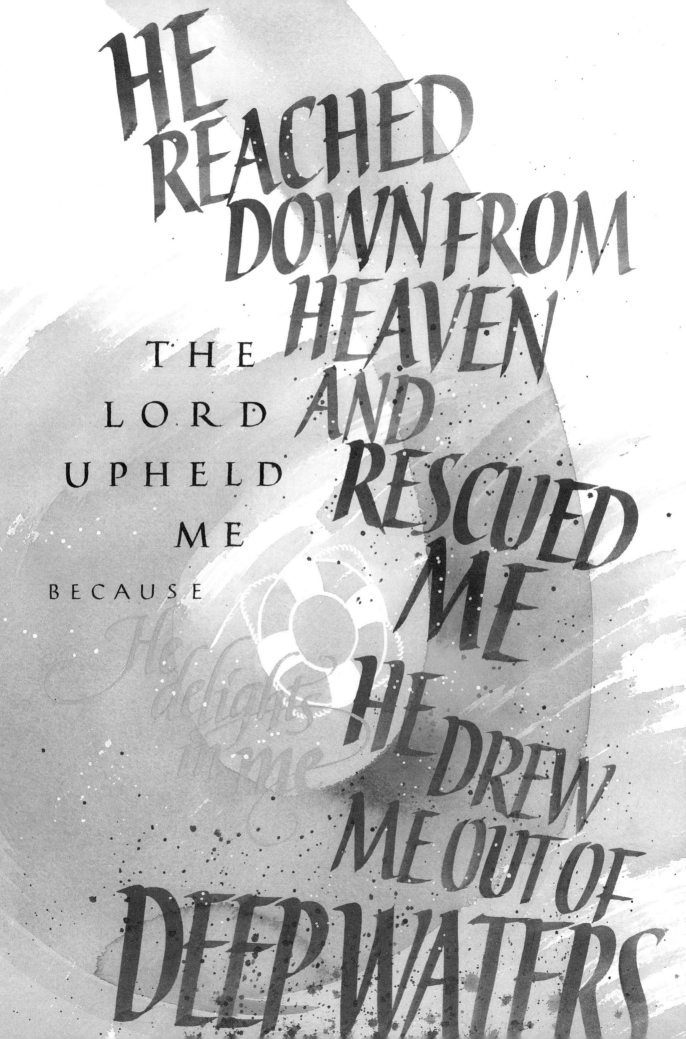

HE
REACHED
DOWN FROM
HEAVEN
AND
RESCUED
ME

THE
LORD
UPHELD
ME

BECAUSE

HE DREW
ME OUT OF
DEEP WATERS

13 Keep me from deliberate sins!
    Don't let them control me.
    Then I will be free of guilt
    and innocent of great sin.

14 May the words of my mouth and the thoughts
        of my heart
    be pleasing to you,
    O LORD, my rock and my redeemer.

## PSALM 20

*For the choir director: A psalm of David.*

1 In times of trouble, may the LORD respond
        to your cry.
    May the God of Israel* keep you safe from
        all harm.
2 May he send you help from his sanctuary
    and strengthen you from Jerusalem.*
3 May he remember all your gifts
    and look favorably on your burnt offerings.
        *Interlude*

4 May he grant your heart's desire
    and fulfill all your plans.
5 May we shout for joy when we hear of your
        victory,
    flying banners to honor our God.
    May the LORD answer all your prayers.

6 Now I know that the LORD saves his anointed
        king.
    He will answer him from his holy heaven
    and rescue him by his great power.
7 Some nations boast of their armies and weapons,*
    but we boast in the LORD our God.
8 Those nations will fall down and collapse,
    but we will rise up and stand firm.

9 Give victory to our king, O LORD!
    Respond to our cry for help.

## PSALM 21

*For the choir director: A psalm of David.*

1 How the king rejoices in your strength,
        O LORD!
    He shouts with joy because of your victory.

2 For you have given him his heart's desire;
    you have held back nothing that he
        requested.    *Interlude*

3 You welcomed him back with success and
        prosperity.
    You placed a crown of finest gold on his head.
4 He asked you to preserve his life,
    and you have granted his request.
    The days of his life stretch on forever.
5 Your victory brings him great honor,
    and you have clothed him with splendor and
        majesty.
6 You have endowed him with eternal blessings.
    You have given him the joy of being in your
        presence.
7 For the king trusts in the LORD.
    The unfailing love of the Most High will
        keep him from stumbling.

8 You will capture all your enemies.
    Your strong right hand will seize all those
        who hate you.
9 You will destroy them as in a flaming furnace
        when you appear.
    The LORD will consume them in his anger;
        fire will devour them.
10 You will wipe their children from the face
        of the earth;
    they will never have descendants.
11 Although they plot against you,
    their evil schemes will never succeed.
12 For they will turn and run
    when they see your arrows aimed at them.

13 We praise you, LORD, for all your glorious
        power.
    With music and singing we celebrate your
        mighty acts.

PSALM 19:1-5   In the ever-changing patterns and colors in the sky, God is showing off his mastery. All peoples in all places have the opportunity to see it—unless we fail to look up. I love seeing the sunset as I leave work during the winter months—especially if the day has been gloomy. The basic elements in artistic composition come right from nature. Here, the rays that emanate from the sun create the basis for my picture.

20:1 Hebrew *of Jacob.*  20:2 Hebrew *Zion.*  20:7 Hebrew *chariots and horses.*

THE SKIES DISPLAY

THE SKIES DISPLAY

THE SKIES DISPLAY

THE HEAVENS TELL OF

the glory of God

HIS MARVELOUS CRAFTSMANSHIP

Their message

has gone out

to all the earth

THE SUN LIVES IN THE HEAVENS

WHERE GOD PLACED IT

IT BURSTS FORTH LIKE A RADIANT BRIDEGROOM

AFTER HIS WEDDING

IT REJOICES LIKE A GREAT ATHLETE

EAGER TO RUN THE RACE

# PSALM 22

*For the choir director: A psalm of David, to be sung to the tune "Doe of the Dawn."*

¹My God, my God! Why have you forsaken me?
    Why do you remain so distant?
    Why do you ignore my cries for help?
²Every day I call to you, my God, but you do
        not answer.
    Every night you hear my voice, but I find
        no relief.

³Yet you are holy.
    The praises of Israel surround your throne.
⁴Our ancestors trusted in you,
    and you rescued them.
⁵You heard their cries for help and saved them.
    They put their trust in you and were never
        disappointed.

⁶But I am a worm and not a man.
    I am scorned and despised by all!
⁷Everyone who sees me mocks me.
    They sneer and shake their heads, saying,
⁸"Is this the one who relies on the LORD?
    Then let the LORD save him!
    If the LORD loves him so much,
        let the LORD rescue him!"

⁹Yet you brought me safely from my mother's
        womb
    and led me to trust you when I was a
        nursing infant.
¹⁰I was thrust upon you at my birth.
    You have been my God from the moment
        I was born.

¹¹Do not stay so far from me,
    for trouble is near,
    and no one else can help me.
¹²My enemies surround me like a herd of bulls;
    fierce bulls of Bashan have hemmed
        me in!
¹³Like roaring lions attacking their prey,
    they come at me with open mouths.
¹⁴My life is poured out like water,
    and all my bones are out of joint.

My heart is like wax,
    melting within me.
¹⁵My strength has dried up like sunbaked clay.
    My tongue sticks to the roof of my mouth.
    You have laid me in the dust and left me for
        dead.

¹⁶My enemies surround me like a pack of dogs;
    an evil gang closes in on me.
    They have pierced my hands and feet.
¹⁷I can count every bone in my body.
    My enemies stare at me and gloat.
¹⁸They divide my clothes among themselves
    and throw dice* for my garments.

¹⁹O LORD, do not stay away!
    You are my strength; come quickly to my
        aid!
²⁰Rescue me from a violent death;
    spare my precious life from these dogs.
²¹Snatch me from the lions' jaws,
    and from the horns of these wild oxen.

²²Then I will declare the wonder of your name
        to my brothers and sisters.
    I will praise you among all your people.
²³Praise the LORD, all you who fear him!
    Honor him, all you descendants of Jacob!
    Show him reverence, all you descendants
        of Israel!
²⁴For he has not ignored the suffering of the
        needy.
    He has not turned and walked away.
    He has listened to their cries for help.

²⁵I will praise you among all the people;
    I will fulfill my vows in the presence of those
        who worship you.
²⁶The poor will eat and be satisfied.
    All who seek the LORD will praise him.
    Their hearts will rejoice with everlasting joy.
²⁷The whole earth will acknowledge the LORD
        and return to him.
    People from every nation will bow down
        before him.
²⁸For the LORD is king!
    He rules all the nations.

**22:18** Hebrew *cast lots.*

²⁹Let the rich of the earth feast and
worship.
Let all mortals—those born to die—bow
down in his presence.
³⁰Future generations will also serve him.
Our children will hear about the wonders
of the Lord.
³¹His righteous acts will be told to those yet
unborn.
They will hear about everything he has done.

## PSALM 23

*A psalm of David.*

¹The LORD is my shepherd;
I have everything I need.
²He lets me rest in green meadows;
he leads me beside peaceful streams.
³ He renews my strength.
He guides me along right paths,
bringing honor to his name.

⁴Even when I walk
through the dark valley of death,*
I will not be afraid,
for you are close beside me.
Your rod and your staff
protect and comfort me.

⁵You prepare a feast for me
in the presence of my enemies.
You welcome me as a guest,
anointing my head with oil.
My cup overflows with blessings.
⁶Surely your goodness and unfailing love will
pursue me
all the days of my life,
and I will live in the house of the LORD
forever.

## PSALM 24

*A psalm of David.*

¹The earth is the LORD's, and everything in it.
The world and all its people belong to him.
²For he laid the earth's foundation on the seas
and built it on the ocean depths.

23:4 Or *the darkest valley.*

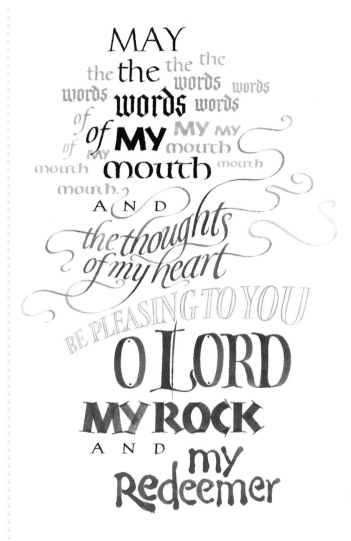

PSALM 19:14  This whole process of interpreting Scripture with calligraphy is very powerful in my own life because it brings me closer to the Lord himself. Daily contact with Scripture protects us from less healthy attitudes around us and checks the myriad of thoughts that go through our mind.

³Who may climb the mountain of the
LORD?
Who may stand in his holy place?
⁴Only those whose hands and hearts are pure,
who do not worship idols
and never tell lies.
⁵They will receive the LORD's blessing
and have right standing with God their
savior.

⁶They alone may enter God's presence
  and worship the God of Israel.*  *Interlude*

⁷Open up, ancient gates!
  Open up, ancient doors,
    and let the King of glory enter.
⁸Who is the King of glory?
  The LORD, strong and mighty,
    the LORD, invincible in battle.
⁹Open up, ancient gates!
  Open up, ancient doors,
    and let the King of glory enter.
¹⁰Who is the King of glory?
  The LORD Almighty—
    he is the King of glory.  *Interlude*

## PSALM 25

*A psalm of David.*

¹To you, O LORD, I lift up my soul.
²  I trust in you, my God!
  Do not let me be disgraced,
    or let my enemies rejoice in my defeat.
³No one who trusts in you will ever be
    disgraced,
  but disgrace comes to those who try to
    deceive others.

⁴Show me the path where I should walk,
    O LORD;
  point out the right road for me to follow.
⁵Lead me by your truth and teach me,
  for you are the God who saves me.
  All day long I put my hope in you.

⁶Remember, O LORD, your unfailing love
    and compassion,
  which you have shown from long ages past.
⁷Forgive the rebellious sins of my youth;
  look instead through the eyes of your
    unfailing love,
  for you are merciful, O LORD.

⁸The LORD is good and does what is right;
  he shows the proper path to those who go
    astray.
⁹He leads the humble in what is right,
  teaching them his way.

¹⁰The LORD leads with unfailing love and
    faithfulness
  all those who keep his covenant and obey his
    decrees.

¹¹For the honor of your name, O LORD,
  forgive my many, many sins.
¹²Who are those who fear the LORD?
  He will show them the path they should
    choose.
¹³They will live in prosperity,
  and their children will inherit the Promised
    Land.
¹⁴Friendship with the LORD is reserved for those
    who fear him.
  With them he shares the secrets of his
    covenant.
¹⁵My eyes are always looking to the LORD for
    help,
  for he alone can rescue me from the traps
    of my enemies.

¹⁶Turn to me and have mercy on me,
  for I am alone and in deep distress.
¹⁷My problems go from bad to worse.
  Oh, save me from them all!
¹⁸Feel my pain and see my trouble.
  Forgive all my sins.
¹⁹See how many enemies I have,
  and how viciously they hate me!
²⁰Protect me! Rescue my life from them!
  Do not let me be disgraced, for I trust
    in you.
²¹May integrity and honesty protect me,
  for I put my hope in you.

²²O God, ransom Israel
  from all its troubles.

PSALM 22:1, 14, 16, 18  These verses are an example of the multiple layers of meaning that are often found in Psalms. Written ten centuries before Christ, they describe remarkably well his suffering and sacrificial death. But people in all times since David can relate to the opening lines, which describe feeling deserted. My experience with the stark simplicity of Japanese art reminded me that this was the place to reduce the design to its bare minimum.

**24:6** Hebrew *of Jacob.*

MY GOD
MY GOD
WHY HAVE YOU
FORSAKEN ME?
my life is poured out
like water
THEY HAVE PIERCED
MY HANDS AND FEET
They divide my clothes
among themselves
and throw d i c e
for my garments

## PSALM 26

*A psalm of David.*

¹Declare me innocent, O LORD,
   for I have acted with integrity;
   I have trusted in the LORD without
      wavering.
²Put me on trial, LORD, and cross-examine me.
   Test my motives and affections.
³For I am constantly aware of your unfailing
      love,
   and I have lived according to your truth.

⁴I do not spend time with liars
   or go along with hypocrites.
⁵I hate the gatherings of those who do evil,
   and I refuse to join in with the wicked.

⁶I wash my hands to declare my innocence.
   I come to your altar, O LORD,
⁷singing a song of thanksgiving
   and telling of all your miracles.
⁸I love your sanctuary, LORD,
   the place where your glory shines.

⁹Don't let me suffer the fate of sinners.
   Don't condemn me along with murderers.
¹⁰Their hands are dirty with wicked schemes,
   and they constantly take bribes.

¹¹But I am not like that; I do what is right.
   So in your mercy, save me.
¹²I have taken a stand,
   and I will publicly praise the LORD.

## PSALM 27

*A psalm of David.*

¹The LORD is my light and my salvation—
   so why should I be afraid?
The LORD protects me from danger—
   so why should I tremble?

²When evil people come to destroy me,
   when my enemies and foes attack me,
   they will stumble and fall.
³Though a mighty army surrounds me,
   my heart will know no fear.
Even if they attack me,
   I remain confident.

⁴The one thing I ask of the LORD—
   the thing I seek most—
is to live in the house of the LORD all the days
      of my life,
   delighting in the LORD's perfections
   and meditating in his Temple.
⁵For he will conceal me there when troubles
      come;
   he will hide me in his sanctuary.
He will place me out of reach on a high rock.
⁶Then I will hold my head high,
   above my enemies who surround me.
At his Tabernacle I will offer sacrifices with
      shouts of joy,
   singing and praising the LORD with music.

⁷Listen to my pleading, O LORD.
   Be merciful and answer me!
⁸My heart has heard you say, "Come and talk
      with me."
   And my heart responds, "LORD, I am
      coming."
⁹Do not hide yourself from me.
   Do not reject your servant in anger.
   You have always been my helper.
Don't leave me now; don't abandon me,
   O God of my salvation!
¹⁰Even if my father and mother abandon me,
   the LORD will hold me close.

¹¹Teach me how to live, O LORD.
   Lead me along the path of honesty,
   for my enemies are waiting for me to fall.
¹²Do not let me fall into their hands.
   For they accuse me of things I've never done
   and breathe out violence against me.
¹³Yet I am confident that I will see the LORD's
      goodness
   while I am here in the land of the living.

✒ PSALM 23:2-6   I am reminded that the Lord has given me everything I need to live. I will sometimes go through hard times, but not alone. Nothing catches the Master by surprise. The shepherd's staff is the dominant symbol here. By enlarging it so that we see only part of it, the crook surrounds the entire text in symbolic mighty protection. All good things come to an end? Not so, says Psalm 23!

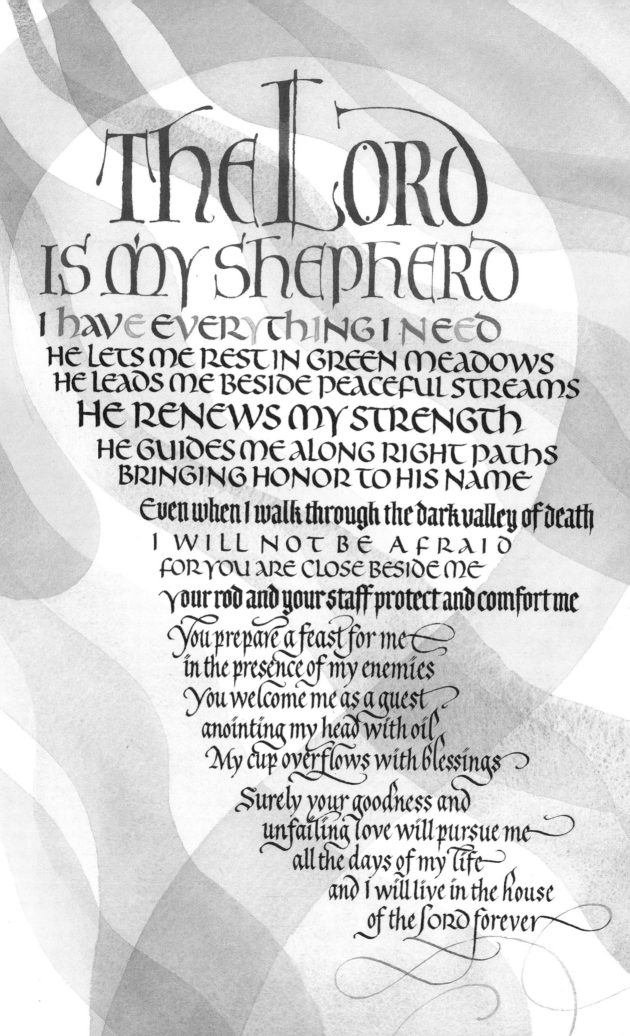

# The Lord
## is my shepherd

I have everything I need
HE LETS ME REST IN GREEN MEADOWS
HE LEADS ME BESIDE PEACEFUL STREAMS
HE RENEWS MY STRENGTH
HE GUIDES ME ALONG RIGHT PATHS
BRINGING HONOR TO HIS NAME

Even when I walk through the dark valley of death
I WILL NOT BE AFRAID
FOR YOU ARE CLOSE BESIDE ME

Your rod and your staff protect and comfort me

You prepare a feast for me
in the presence of my enemies
You welcome me as a guest
anointing my head with oil
My cup overflows with blessings

Surely your goodness and
unfailing love will pursue me
all the days of my life
and I will live in the house
of the Lord forever

14 Wait patiently for the LORD.
    Be brave and courageous.
    Yes, wait patiently for the LORD.

## PSALM 28

*A psalm of David.*

1 O LORD, you are my rock of safety.
    Please help me; don't refuse to answer me.
  For if you are silent,
    I might as well give up and die.
2 Listen to my prayer for mercy
    as I cry out to you for help,
    as I lift my hands toward your holy sanctuary.

3 Don't drag me away with the wicked—
    with those who do evil—
  those who speak friendly words to their
      neighbors
    while planning evil in their hearts.
4 Give them the punishment they so richly
      deserve!
    Measure it out in proportion to their
      wickedness.
  Pay them back for all their evil deeds!
    Give them a taste of what they have done
      to others.
5 They care nothing for what the LORD has done
    or for what his hands have made.
  So he will tear them down like old buildings,
    and they will never be rebuilt!

6 Praise the LORD!
    For he has heard my cry for mercy.
7 The LORD is my strength, my shield from
      every danger.
    I trust in him with all my heart.
  He helps me, and my heart is filled with joy.
    I burst out in songs of thanksgiving.

8 The LORD protects his people
    and gives victory to his anointed king.
9 Save your people!
    Bless Israel, your special possession!
  Lead them like a shepherd,
    and carry them forever in your arms.

## PSALM 29

*A psalm of David.*

1 Give honor to the LORD, you angels;
    give honor to the LORD for his glory and
      strength.
2 Give honor to the LORD for the glory of his
      name.
    Worship the LORD in the splendor of his
      holiness.

3 The voice of the LORD echoes above
      the sea.
    The God of glory thunders.
    The LORD thunders over the mighty sea.
4 The voice of the LORD is powerful;
    the voice of the LORD is full of majesty.
5 The voice of the LORD splits the mighty cedars;
    the LORD shatters the cedars of Lebanon.
6 He makes Lebanon's mountains skip like a calf
    and Mount Hermon* to leap like a young
      bull.
7 The voice of the LORD strikes with lightning
      bolts.
8 The voice of the LORD makes the desert
      quake;
    the LORD shakes the desert of Kadesh.
9 The voice of the LORD twists mighty oaks*
    and strips the forests bare.
  In his Temple everyone shouts, "Glory!"

10 The LORD rules over the floodwaters.
    The LORD reigns as king forever.
11 The LORD gives his people strength.
    The LORD blesses them with peace.

## PSALM 30

*A psalm of David, sung at the dedication of the Temple.*

1 I will praise you, LORD, for you have rescued me.
    You refused to let my enemies triumph
      over me.
2 O LORD my God, I cried out to you for help,
    and you restored my health.
3 You brought me up from the grave, O LORD.
    You kept me from falling into the pit
      of death.

**29:6** Hebrew *Sirion,* another name for Mount Hermon. **29:9** Or *causes the deer to writhe in labor.*

⁴Sing to the LORD, all you godly ones!
    Praise his holy name.
⁵His anger lasts for a moment,
    but his favor lasts a lifetime!
Weeping may go on all night,
    but joy comes with the morning.

⁶When I was prosperous I said,
    "Nothing can stop me now!"
⁷Your favor, O LORD, made me as secure as
    a mountain.
    Then you turned away from me, and I was
    shattered.

⁸I cried out to you, O LORD.
    I begged the Lord for mercy, saying,
⁹"What will you gain if I die,
    if I sink down into the grave?
Can my dust praise you from the grave?
    Can it tell the world of your faithfulness?
¹⁰Hear me, LORD, and have mercy on me.
    Help me, O LORD."

¹¹You have turned my mourning into joyful
    dancing.
    You have taken away my clothes of
    mourning and clothed me with joy,
¹²that I might sing praises to you and not be
    silent.
    O LORD my God, I will give you thanks
    forever!

## PSALM 31

*For the choir director: A psalm of David.*

¹O LORD, I have come to you for protection;
    don't let me be put to shame.
    Rescue me, for you always do what is right.
²Bend down and listen to me;
    rescue me quickly.
Be for me a great rock of safety,
    a fortress where my enemies cannot reach me.

³You are my rock and my fortress.
    For the honor of your name, lead me out
    of this peril.
⁴Pull me from the trap my enemies set for me,
    for I find protection in you alone.

THE LORD IS MY LIGHT and my salvation so why should I be afraid?

PSALM 27:1   The Lord saves me from death and rescues me from the evil all around me. So I don't need to withdraw from society. Light through a prism yields the purest colors. All other things pale in comparison to God's splendor. So unlike most of my more muted color schemes, I avoided mixing complementary colors in this piece.

⁵I entrust my spirit into your hand.
    Rescue me, LORD, for you are a faithful God.

⁶I hate those who worship worthless idols.
    I trust in the LORD.
⁷I am overcome with joy because of your
    unfailing love,
    for you have seen my troubles,
    and you care about the anguish of my soul.

8 You have not handed me over to my enemy
    but have set me in a safe place.

9 Have mercy on me, LORD, for I am in distress.
    My sight is blurred because of my tears.
    My body and soul are withering away.
10 I am dying from grief;
    my years are shortened by sadness.
    Misery★ has drained my strength;
    I am wasting away from within.
11 I am scorned by all my enemies
    and despised by my neighbors—
    even my friends are afraid to come near me.
    When they see me on the street,
    they turn the other way.
12 I have been ignored as if I were dead,
    as if I were a broken pot.
13 I have heard the many rumors about me,
    and I am surrounded by terror.
    My enemies conspire against me,
    plotting to take my life.

14 But I am trusting you, O LORD,
    saying, "You are my God!"
15 My future is in your hands.
    Rescue me from those who hunt me down
    relentlessly.
16 Let your favor shine on your servant.
    In your unfailing love, save me.
17 Don't let me be disgraced, O LORD,
    for I call out to you for help.
    Let the wicked be disgraced;
    let them lie silent in the grave.
18 May their lying lips be silenced—
    those proud and arrogant lips that accuse the
    godly.

19 Your goodness is so great!
    You have stored up great blessings for those
    who honor you.
    You have done so much for those who come
    to you for protection,
    blessing them before the watching world.
20 You hide them in the shelter of your presence,
    safe from those who conspire against them.
    You shelter them in your presence,
    far from accusing tongues.

21 Praise the LORD,
    for he has shown me his unfailing love.
    He kept me safe when my city was under
    attack.
22 In sudden fear I had cried out,
    "I have been cut off from the LORD!"
    But you heard my cry for mercy
    and answered my call for help.
23 Love the LORD, all you faithful ones!
    For the LORD protects those who are loyal
    to him,
    but he harshly punishes all who are
    arrogant.
24 So be strong and take courage,
    all you who put your hope in the LORD!

## PSALM 32

*A psalm of David.*

1 Oh, what joy for those
    whose rebellion is forgiven,
    whose sin is put out of sight!
2 Yes, what joy for those
    whose record the LORD has cleared
    of sin,
    whose lives are lived in complete honesty!
3 When I refused to confess my sin,
    I was weak and miserable,
    and I groaned all day long.
4 Day and night your hand of discipline was
    heavy on me.
    My strength evaporated like water in the
    summer heat.      *Interlude*

5 Finally, I confessed all my sins to you
    and stopped trying to hide them.
    I said to myself, "I will confess my rebellion
    to the LORD."

PSALM 29:2-3, 5, 8   In addition to all the *sights* around us, *sounds* also display God's power and glory. To make a picture of sound, artists use a variety of textures, patterns, and colors—often in repetition. One of my favorite compliments came from a deaf friend who told me that through my interpretations of musical texts I helped her experience what music must be like!

31:10 Or *Sin.*

THE VOICE OF THE LORD

ECHOES ABOVE

ECHOES ABOVE THE SEA

ECHOES ABOVE THE SE

THE GOD OF GLORY THUNDERS

THUNDERS
THUNDERS
THUNDERS

Worship the Lord in the splendor of his holiness

THE VOICE OF THE LORD

THE VOICE OF THE LORD SPLITS THE MIGHTY CEDARS

THE VOICE OF THE LORD MAKES THE DESERT QUAKE

QUAKE QUAKE
QUAKE QUAKE
QUAKE QUAKE
QUAKE QUAKE QUA
QUAKE
QUAKE QUAKE

And you forgave me! All my guilt is gone.
*Interlude*

6 Therefore, let all the godly confess their
rebellion to you while there is time,
that they may not drown in the floodwaters
of judgment.
7 For you are my hiding place;
you protect me from trouble.
You surround me with songs of victory.
*Interlude*

8 The LORD says, "I will guide you along the
best pathway for your life.
I will advise you and watch over you.
9 Do not be like a senseless horse or mule
that needs a bit and bridle to keep it under
control."

10 Many sorrows come to the wicked,
but unfailing love surrounds those who trust
the LORD.
11 So rejoice in the LORD and be glad, all you
who obey him!
Shout for joy, all you whose hearts are
pure!

## PSALM 33

1 Let the godly sing with joy to the LORD,
for it is fitting to praise him.
2 Praise the LORD with melodies on the lyre;
make music for him on the ten-stringed
harp.
3 Sing new songs of praise to him;
play skillfully on the harp and sing
with joy.

4 For the word of the LORD holds true,
and everything he does is worthy of our
trust.
5 He loves whatever is just and good,
and his unfailing love fills the earth.

6 The LORD merely spoke,
and the heavens were created.
He breathed the word,
and all the stars were born.
7 He gave the sea its boundaries
and locked the oceans in vast reservoirs.

8 Let everyone in the world fear the LORD,
and let everyone stand in awe of him.
9 For when he spoke, the world began!
It appeared at his command.

10 The LORD shatters the plans of the nations
and thwarts all their schemes.
11 But the LORD's plans stand firm forever;
his intentions can never be shaken.

12 What joy for the nation whose God is the
LORD,
whose people he has chosen for his own.

13 The LORD looks down from heaven
and sees the whole human race.
14 From his throne he observes
all who live on the earth.
15 He made their hearts,
so he understands everything they do.
16 The best-equipped army cannot save a king,
nor is great strength enough to save a warrior.
17 Don't count on your warhorse to give you
victory—
for all its strength, it cannot save you.

18 But the LORD watches over those who fear
him,
those who rely on his unfailing love.
19 He rescues them from death
and keeps them alive in times of famine.

20 We depend on the LORD alone to save us.
Only he can help us, protecting us like a
shield.
21 In him our hearts rejoice,
for we are trusting in his holy name.
22 Let your unfailing love surround us, LORD,
for our hope is in you alone.

## PSALM 34

*A psalm of David, regarding the time he pretended to be
insane in front of Abimelech, who sent him away.*

1 I will praise the LORD at all times.
I will constantly speak his praises.
2 I will boast only in the LORD;
let all who are discouraged take heart.
3 Come, let us tell of the LORD's greatness;
let us exalt his name together.

⁴I prayed to the LORD, and he answered me,
    freeing me from all my fears.
⁵Those who look to him for help will be
    radiant with joy;
    no shadow of shame will darken their
    faces.
⁶I cried out to the LORD in my suffering,
    and he heard me.
    He set me free from all my fears.
⁷For the angel of the LORD guards all who
    fear him,
    and he rescues them.

⁸Taste and see that the LORD is good.
    Oh, the joys of those who trust in him!
⁹Let the LORD's people show him reverence,
    for those who honor him will have all they
    need.
¹⁰Even strong young lions sometimes go
    hungry,
    but those who trust in the LORD will
    never lack any good thing.

¹¹Come, my children, and listen to me,
    and I will teach you to fear the LORD.
¹²Do any of you want to live
    a life that is long and good?
¹³Then watch your tongue!
    Keep your lips from telling lies!
¹⁴Turn away from evil and do good.
    Work hard at living in peace with others.

¹⁵The eyes of the LORD watch over those who
    do right;
    his ears are open to their cries for help.
¹⁶But the LORD turns his face against those
    who do evil;
    he will erase their memory from the
    earth.

¹⁷The LORD hears his people when they call
    to him for help.
    He rescues them from all their troubles.
¹⁸The LORD is close to the brokenhearted;
    he rescues those who are crushed in spirit.

¹⁹The righteous face many troubles,
    but the LORD rescues them from each and
    every one.

Weeping may go on all night

BUT JOY comes with the morning

✎ PSALM 30:5  We learn in this psalm that there
are times for both sorrow and joy. There was an unre-
solved tension in my first sketch because I treated both
halves of the verse equally. Although the sorrow seems
to occupy the longest time period, I decided to emphasize the joy. The direction of the letter strokes also
illustrates the verse's contrast: downward in the first
part and upward in the climax.

²⁰For the LORD protects them from harm—
    not one of their bones will be broken!

²¹Calamity will surely overtake the wicked,
    and those who hate the righteous will be
    punished.
²²But the LORD will redeem those who serve him.
    Everyone who trusts in him will be freely
    pardoned.

# PSALM 35

*A psalm of David.*

¹ O LORD, oppose those who oppose me.
Declare war on those who are attacking me.
² Put on your armor, and take up your shield.
Prepare for battle, and come to my aid.
³ Lift up your spear and javelin
and block the way of my enemies.
Let me hear you say,
"I am your salvation!"

⁴ Humiliate and disgrace those trying to
kill me;
turn them back in confusion.
⁵ Blow them away like chaff in the wind—
a wind sent by the angel of the LORD.
⁶ Make their path dark and slippery,
with the angel of the LORD pursuing them.
⁷ Although I did them no wrong,
they laid a trap for me.
Although I did them no wrong,
they dug a pit for me.
⁸ So let sudden ruin overtake them!
Let them be caught in the snare they set
for me!
Let them fall to destruction in the pit they
dug for me.

⁹ Then I will rejoice in the LORD.
I will be glad because he rescues me.
¹⁰ I will praise him from the bottom of my
heart:
"LORD, who can compare with you?
Who else rescues the weak and helpless from
the strong?
Who else protects the poor and needy from
those who want to rob them?"

¹¹ Malicious witnesses testify against me.
They accuse me of things I don't even know
about.
¹² They repay me with evil for the good I do.
I am sick with despair.
¹³ Yet when they were ill,
I grieved for them.
I even fasted and prayed for them,
but my prayers returned unanswered.

¹⁴ I was sad, as though they were my friends
or family,
as if I were grieving for my own mother.

¹⁵ But they are glad now that I am in trouble;
they gleefully join together against me.
I am attacked by people I don't even know;
they hurl slander at me continually.
¹⁶ They mock me with the worst kind of profanity,
and they snarl at me.

¹⁷ How long, O Lord, will you look on and
do nothing?
Rescue me from their fierce attacks.
Protect my life from these lions!
¹⁸ Then I will thank you in front of the entire
congregation.
I will praise you before all the people.

¹⁹ Don't let my treacherous enemies
rejoice over my defeat.
Don't let those who hate me without cause
gloat over my sorrow.
²⁰ They don't talk of peace;
they plot against innocent people
who are minding their own business.
²¹ They shout that they have seen me doing wrong.
"Aha," they say. "Aha!
With our own eyes we saw him do it!"

²² O LORD, you know all about this.
Do not stay silent.
Don't abandon me now, O Lord.
²³ Wake up! Rise to my defense!
Take up my case, my God and my Lord.
²⁴ Declare me "not guilty," O LORD my God,
for you give justice.
Don't let my enemies laugh about me in
my troubles.
²⁵ Don't let them say, "Look! We have what we
wanted!
Now we will eat him alive!"

✒ PSALM 33:12 Throughout Scripture, God makes known his intention to be for all peoples. Using symbols of different cultures seemed to be the natural way to picture the celebration in these words. As in real life, the challenge here was to take all this diversity and bring it together harmoniously.

²⁶May those who rejoice at my troubles
　　be humiliated and disgraced.
　May those who triumph over me
　　be covered with shame and dishonor.

²⁷But give great joy to those
　　who have stood with me in my defense.
　Let them continually say, "Great is the LORD,
　　who enjoys helping his servant."
²⁸Then I will tell everyone of your justice and
　　goodness,
　　and I will praise you all day long.

## PSALM 36

*For the choir director: A psalm of David, the servant
of the LORD.*

¹Sin whispers to the wicked, deep within their
　　hearts.
　They have no fear of God to restrain them.
²In their blind conceit,
　　they cannot see how wicked they really are.
³Everything they say is crooked and deceitful.
　　They refuse to act wisely or do what is good.
⁴They lie awake at night, hatching sinful plots.
　　Their course of action is never good.
　They make no attempt to turn from evil.

⁵Your unfailing love, O LORD, is as vast as the
　　heavens;
　　your faithfulness reaches beyond the clouds.
⁶Your righteousness is like the mighty
　　mountains,
　　your justice like the ocean depths.
　You care for people and animals alike, O LORD.
⁷　How precious is your unfailing love, O God!
　All humanity finds shelter
　　in the shadow of your wings.
⁸You feed them from the abundance of your
　　own house,
　　letting them drink from your rivers of
　　delight.
⁹For you are the fountain of life,
　　the light by which we see.

¹⁰Pour out your unfailing love on those who
　　love you;
　　give justice to those with honest hearts.

¹¹Don't let the proud trample me;
　　don't let the wicked push me around.
¹²Look! They have fallen!
　　They have been thrown down, never to rise
　　again.

## PSALM 37

*A psalm of David.*

¹Don't worry about the wicked.
　　Don't envy those who do wrong.
²For like grass, they soon fade away.
　　Like springtime flowers, they soon wither.

³Trust in the LORD and do good.
　　Then you will live safely in the land and
　　prosper.
⁴Take delight in the LORD,
　　and he will give you your heart's desires.

⁵Commit everything you do to the LORD.
　　Trust him, and he will help you.
⁶He will make your innocence as clear as the
　　dawn,
　　and the justice of your cause will shine
　　like the noonday sun.

⁷Be still in the presence of the LORD,
　　and wait patiently for him to act.
　Don't worry about evil people who prosper
　　or fret about their wicked schemes.

⁸Stop your anger!
　　Turn from your rage!
　Do not envy others—
　　it only leads to harm.
⁹For the wicked will be destroyed,
　　but those who trust in the LORD will possess
　　the land.

¹⁰In a little while, the wicked will disappear.
　　Though you look for them, they will be gone.
¹¹Those who are gentle and lowly will possess
　　the land;
　　they will live in prosperous security.

¹²The wicked plot against the godly;
　　they snarl at them in defiance.
¹³But the Lord just laughs,
　　for he sees their day of judgment coming.

14 The wicked draw their swords
   and string their bows
 to kill the poor and the oppressed,
   to slaughter those who do right.
15 But they will be stabbed through the heart
   with their own swords,
   and their bows will be broken.

16 It is better to be godly and have little
   than to be evil and possess much.
17 For the strength of the wicked will be
   shattered,
   but the LORD takes care of the godly.

18 Day by day the LORD takes care of the
   innocent,
   and they will receive a reward that lasts
   forever.
19 They will survive through hard times;
   even in famine they will have more than
   enough.

20 But the wicked will perish.
   The LORD's enemies are like flowers in a
   field—
   they will disappear like smoke.

21 The wicked borrow and never repay,
   but the godly are generous givers.
22 Those blessed by the LORD will inherit the
   land,
   but those cursed by him will die.

23 The steps of the godly are directed by the
   LORD.
   He delights in every detail of their lives.
24 Though they stumble, they will not fall,
   for the LORD holds them by the hand.

25 Once I was young, and now I am old.
   Yet I have never seen the godly forsaken,
   nor seen their children begging for bread.
26 The godly always give generous loans to
   others,
   and their children are a blessing.

27 Turn from evil and do good,
   and you will live in the land forever.
28 For the LORD loves justice,
   and he will never abandon the godly.

PSALM 34:8  I wanted to suggest a rich selection of sweet fruits clustered together. Since the verse is really about God's goodness in a broader sense, I refrained from drawing fruit from nature. Subtlety in art is meant to engage the viewer's own imagination. For the flourishes I changed to a smaller pen so that they would not detract from the words themselves. Perhaps you're wondering how the different colors were written. First I penciled in the words. Then I wrote all the letters of one color at a time.

He will keep them safe forever,
  but the children of the wicked will perish.
²⁹ The godly will inherit the land
  and will live there forever.

³⁰ The godly offer good counsel;
  they know what is right from wrong.
³¹ They fill their hearts with God's law,
  so they will never slip from his path.

³² Those who are evil spy on the godly,
  waiting for an excuse to kill them.
³³ But the LORD will not let the wicked succeed
  or let the godly be condemned when they
    are brought before the judge.

³⁴ Don't be impatient for the LORD to act!
  Travel steadily along his path.
  He will honor you, giving you the land.
  You will see the wicked destroyed.

³⁵ I myself have seen it happen—
  proud and evil people thriving like mighty
    trees.
³⁶ But when I looked again, they were gone!
  Though I searched for them, I could not
    find them!

³⁷ Look at those who are honest and good,
  for a wonderful future lies before those who
    love peace.
³⁸ But the wicked will be destroyed;
  they have no future.

³⁹ The LORD saves the godly;
  he is their fortress in times of trouble.
⁴⁰ The LORD helps them,
  rescuing them from the wicked.
  He saves them,
  and they find shelter in him.

## PSALM 38

*A psalm of David, to bring us to the LORD's remembrance.*

¹ O LORD, don't rebuke me in your anger!
  Don't discipline me in your rage!
² Your arrows have struck deep,
  and your blows are crushing me.

³ Because of your anger, my whole body is sick;
  my health is broken because of my sins.
⁴ My guilt overwhelms me—
  it is a burden too heavy to bear.
⁵ My wounds fester and stink
  because of my foolish sins.
⁶ I am bent over and racked with pain.
  My days are filled with grief.
⁷ A raging fever burns within me,
  and my health is broken.
⁸ I am exhausted and completely crushed.
  My groans come from an anguished heart.

⁹ You know what I long for, Lord;
  you hear my every sigh.
¹⁰ My heart beats wildly, my strength fails,
  and I am going blind.
¹¹ My loved ones and friends stay away, fearing
    my disease.
  Even my own family stands at a distance.
¹² Meanwhile, my enemies lay traps for me;
  they make plans to ruin me.
  They think up treacherous deeds all day long.
¹³ But I am deaf to all their threats.
  I am silent before them as one who cannot
    speak.
¹⁴ I choose to hear nothing,
  and I make no reply.

¹⁵ For I am waiting for you, O LORD.
  You must answer for me, O Lord my God.
¹⁶ I prayed, "Don't let my enemies gloat over me
  or rejoice at my downfall."
¹⁷ I am on the verge of collapse,
  facing constant pain.
¹⁸ But I confess my sins;
  I am deeply sorry for what I have done.
¹⁹ My enemies are many;
  they hate me though I have done nothing
    against them.

🖋 PSALM 36:5-6, 9  The strength of visual imagery is that it helps us to experience meaning more deeply. Besides creating life, God is the energy and vitality behind it. The principle of repetition is used here to echo the continual cycles of renewal and reproduction we witness around us. On another level, it represents the rejuvenation of our spirit following dry times.

20 They repay me evil for good
and oppose me because I stand for the right.

21 Do not abandon me, LORD.
Do not stand at a distance, my God.
22 Come quickly to help me, O Lord my savior.

## PSALM 39

*For Jeduthun, the choir director: A psalm of David.*

1 I said to myself, "I will watch what I do
and not sin in what I say.
I will curb my tongue
when the ungodly are around me."
2 But as I stood there in silence—
not even speaking of good things—
the turmoil within me grew to the bursting
point.
3 My thoughts grew hot within me
and began to burn,
igniting a fire of words:
4 "LORD, remind me how brief my time on
earth will be.
Remind me that my days are numbered,
and that my life is fleeing away.
5 My life is no longer than the width of my
hand.
An entire lifetime is just a moment to you;
human existence is but a breath."        *Interlude*

6 We are merely moving shadows,
and all our busy rushing ends in nothing.
We heap up wealth for someone else to
spend.

7 And so, Lord, where do I put my hope?
My only hope is in you.
8 Rescue me from my rebellion,
for even fools mock me when I rebel.
9 I am silent before you; I won't say a word.
For my punishment is from you.
10 Please, don't punish me anymore!
I am exhausted by the blows from your hand.
11 When you discipline people for their sins,
their lives can be crushed like the life
of a moth.
Human existence is as frail as breath.
        *Interlude*

12 Hear my prayer, O LORD!
Listen to my cries for help!
Don't ignore my tears.
For I am your guest—
a traveler passing through,
as my ancestors were before me.
13 Spare me so I can smile again
before I am gone and exist no more.

## PSALM 40

*For the choir director: A psalm of David.*

1 I waited patiently for the LORD to help me,
and he turned to me and heard my cry.
2 He lifted me out of the pit of despair,
out of the mud and the mire.
He set my feet on solid ground
and steadied me as I walked along.
3 He has given me a new song to sing,
a hymn of praise to our God.
Many will see what he has done and be
astounded.
They will put their trust in the LORD.

4 Oh, the joys of those who trust the LORD,
who have no confidence in the proud,
or in those who worship idols.
5 O LORD my God, you have done many
miracles for us.
Your plans for us are too numerous
to list.
If I tried to recite all your wonderful deeds,
I would never come to the end of them.

6 You take no delight in sacrifices or offerings.
Now that you have made me listen, I finally
understand—
you don't require burnt offerings or sin
offerings.
7 Then I said, "Look, I have come.
And this has been written about me in your
scroll:

✐ PSALM 37:23-24   The shoeprints symbolize
for me that God prepares us well for life's journey
when we trust him. Notice the contrasts I used in
letter styles to bring out the meanings of these three
distinct ideas: light and dark, giant and tiny, regimented
and playful.

TAKE

COMMIT

THE STEPS OF THE GODLY

ARE DIRECTED BY THE LORD

EVERYTHING

delight

in the LORD

and he will

HE DELIGHTS IN EVERY DETAIL OF THEIR LIVES

YOU DO

THE LORD

TO THE LORD

THOUGH THEY STUMBLE

TRUST HIM

GIVE YOU

THOUGH THEY WILL NOT FALL

AND HE WILL

your heart's

FOR THE LORD HOLDS THEM

HELP YOU

desires

BY THE HAND

⁸I take joy in doing your will, my God,
for your law is written on my heart."

⁹I have told all your people about your justice.
I have not been afraid to speak out,
as you, O LORD, well know.

¹⁰I have not kept this good news hidden in my
heart;
I have talked about your faithfulness and
saving power.
I have told everyone in the great assembly
of your unfailing love and faithfulness.

¹¹LORD, don't hold back your tender mercies
from me.
My only hope is in your unfailing love and
faithfulness.

¹²For troubles surround me—
too many to count!
They pile up so high
I can't see my way out.
They are more numerous than the hairs on
my head.
I have lost all my courage.

¹³Please, LORD, rescue me!
Come quickly, LORD, and help me.

¹⁴May those who try to destroy me
be humiliated and put to shame.
May those who take delight in my trouble
be turned back in disgrace.

¹⁵Let them be horrified by their shame,
for they said, "Aha! We've got him now!"

¹⁶But may all who search for you
be filled with joy and gladness.
May those who love your salvation
repeatedly shout, "The LORD is great!"

¹⁷As for me, I am poor and needy,
but the Lord is thinking about me right now.
You are my helper and my savior.
Do not delay, O my God.

## PSALM 41

*For the choir director: A psalm of David.*

¹Oh, the joys of those who are kind to the poor.
The LORD rescues them in times of trouble.

²The LORD protects them
and keeps them alive.
He gives them prosperity
and rescues them from their enemies.

³The LORD nurses them when they are sick
and eases their pain and discomfort.

⁴"O LORD," I prayed, "have mercy on me.
Heal me, for I have sinned against you."

⁵But my enemies say nothing but evil
about me.
"How soon will he die and be forgotten?"
they ask.

⁶They visit me as if they are my friends,
but all the while they gather gossip,
and when they leave, they spread it
everywhere.

⁷All who hate me whisper about me,
imagining the worst for me.

⁸"Whatever he has, it is fatal," they say.
"He will never get out of that bed!"

⁹Even my best friend, the one I trusted
completely,
the one who shared my food,
has turned against me.

¹⁰LORD, have mercy on me.
Make me well again, so I can pay them
back!

¹¹I know that you are pleased with me,
for you have not let my enemy triumph
over me.

¹²You have preserved my life because I am
innocent;
you have brought me into your presence
forever.

¹³Bless the LORD, the God of Israel,
who lives forever from eternal ages past.
Amen and amen!

✎ PSALM 38:3-4, 6, 9-11, 18, 22   Writing the
words in layers is not meant to take away from their
importance. Rather, the overlapping text is intended
to represent its sorrowful mood. This is much like when
we pour out our heart to God—we are not always
coherent or eloquent. For me there is more integrity in
my work if you can feel the pain of the words through
what you see.

My guilt

My health is broken

Overwhelms me

because of my sins

My days are filled with grief

It is a burden too heavy to bear

You know what I long for, Lord

You hear my every sigh

My heart beats wildly

My strength fails

BUT

I CONFESS MY SINS

I AM DEEPLY SORRY FOR WHAT I HAVE DONE

COME QUICKLY TO HELP ME

O LORD MY SAVIOR

BOOK TWO (Psalms 42–72)

## PSALM 42

*For the choir director: A psalm of the descendants of Korah.*

¹As the deer pants for streams of water,
    so I long for you, O God.
²I thirst for God, the living God.
    When can I come and stand before him?
³Day and night, I have only tears for food,
    while my enemies continually taunt me,
        saying,
    "Where is this God of yours?"

⁴My heart is breaking
    as I remember how it used to be:
I walked among the crowds of worshipers,
    leading a great procession to the house of
        God,
singing for joy and giving thanks—
    it was the sound of a great celebration!

⁵Why am I discouraged?
    Why so sad?
I will put my hope in God!
    I will praise him again—
        my Savior and ⁶my God!

Now I am deeply discouraged,
    but I will remember your kindness—
from Mount Hermon, the source of the Jordan,
    from the land of Mount Mizar.
⁷I hear the tumult of the raging seas
    as your waves and surging tides sweep
        over me.

⁸Through each day the LORD pours his
        unfailing love upon me,
    and through each night I sing his songs,
        praying to God who gives me life.

⁹"O God my rock," I cry,
    "Why have you forsaken me?
Why must I wander in darkness,
    oppressed by my enemies?"
¹⁰Their taunts pierce me like a fatal wound.
    They scoff, "Where is this God of yours?"

¹¹Why am I discouraged?
    Why so sad?

I will put my hope in God!
    I will praise him again—
        my Savior and my God!

## PSALM 43

¹O God, take up my cause!
    Defend me against these ungodly
        people.
    Rescue me from these unjust liars.
²For you are God, my only safe haven.
    Why have you tossed me aside?
Why must I wander around in darkness,
    oppressed by my enemies?

³Send out your light and your truth;
    let them guide me.
Let them lead me to your holy mountain,
    to the place where you live.
⁴There I will go to the altar of God,
    to God—the source of all my joy.
I will praise you with my harp,
    O God, my God!

⁵Why am I discouraged?
    Why so sad?
I will put my hope in God!
    I will praise him again—
        my Savior and my God!

## PSALM 44

*For the choir director: A psalm of the descendants of Korah.*

¹O God, we have heard it with our own
        ears—
    our ancestors have told us
of all you did in other days,
    in days long ago:
²You drove out the pagan nations
    and gave all the land to our ancestors;
you crushed their enemies,
    setting our ancestors free.

✒ PSALM 39:4-7 The psalmist understands that apart from the Lord, life is futile. The realization that we are dying, coupled with the hope of life beyond the grave, is the basis for the double human image. The words here are kept small in proportion to the whole page to portray the fragility of which they speak.

# LORD

remind me how brief
my time on earth will be
remind me that my days are numbered
and that my life is f l e e i n g  a w a y
my life is no longer than the width of my hand

A N   E N T I R E   L I F E T I M E

is just a moment to you
human existence is but a breath

We are merely moving shadows

and all our busy rushing ends in n o t h i n g
all our busy rushing
our busy rushing

We heap up wealth for someone else
to spend

A N D   S O   L O R D
Where do I put my hope?

# MY ONLY HOPE
## IS IN YOU

³They did not conquer the land with their
swords;
    it was not their own strength that gave them
    victory.
  It was by your mighty power that they
  succeeded;
    it was because you favored them and smiled
    on them.

⁴You are my King and my God.
    You command victories for your people.*
⁵Only by your power can we push back our
enemies;
    only in your name can we trample our foes.
⁶I do not trust my bow;
    I do not count on my sword to save me.
⁷It is you who gives us victory over our
enemies;
    it is you who humbles those who hate us.
⁸O God, we give glory to you all day long
    and constantly praise your name.    *Interlude*

⁹But now you have tossed us aside in dishonor.
    You no longer lead our armies to battle.
¹⁰You make us retreat from our enemies
    and allow them to plunder our land.
¹¹You have treated us like sheep waiting
    to be slaughtered;
    you have scattered us among the nations.
¹²You sold us—your precious people—
    for a pittance.
    You valued us at nothing at all.

¹³You have caused all our neighbors to mock us.
    We are an object of scorn and derision to the
    nations around us.
¹⁴You have made us the butt of their jokes;
    we are scorned by the whole world.
¹⁵We can't escape the constant humiliation;
    shame is written across our faces.
¹⁶All we hear are the taunts of our mockers.
    All we see are our vengeful enemies.

¹⁷All this has happened despite our loyalty to you.
    We have not violated your covenant.
¹⁸Our hearts have not deserted you.
    We have not strayed from your path.

¹⁹Yet you have crushed us in the desert.
    You have covered us with darkness and
    death.

²⁰If we had turned away from worshiping
our God
    or spread our hands in prayer to foreign gods,
²¹God would surely have known it,
    for he knows the secrets of every heart.
²²For your sake we are killed every day;
    we are being slaughtered like sheep.

²³Wake up, O Lord! Why do you sleep?
    Get up! Do not reject us forever.
²⁴Why do you look the other way?
    Why do you ignore our suffering and
    oppression?
²⁵We collapse in the dust,
    lying face down in the dirt.
²⁶Rise up! Come and help us!
    Save us because of your unfailing love.

## PSALM 45

*For the choir director: A psalm of the descendants of
Korah, to be sung to the tune "Lilies." A love song.*

¹My heart overflows with a beautiful thought!
    I will recite a lovely poem to the king,
    for my tongue is like the pen of a skillful
    poet.

²You are the most handsome of all.
    Gracious words stream from your lips.
    God himself has blessed you forever.
³Put on your sword, O mighty warrior!
    You are so glorious, so majestic!
⁴In your majesty, ride out to victory,
    defending truth, humility, and justice.
    Go forth to perform awe-inspiring deeds!
⁵Your arrows are sharp,
    piercing your enemies' hearts.
  The nations fall before you,
    lying down beneath your feet.

⁶Your throne, O God,* endures forever and ever.
    Your royal power is expressed in justice.
⁷You love what is right and hate what is wrong.
    Therefore God, your God, has anointed you,

44:4 Hebrew *for Jacob.*  45:6 Or *Your divine throne.*

pouring out the oil of joy on you more than
on anyone else.
⁸Your robes are perfumed with myrrh, aloes,
and cassia.
In palaces decorated with ivory,
you are entertained by the music of harps.
⁹Kings' daughters are among your concubines.
At your right side stands the queen,
wearing jewelry of finest gold from Ophir!

¹⁰Listen to me, O royal daughter; take to heart
what I say.
Forget your people and your homeland far
away.
¹¹For your royal husband delights in your
beauty;
honor him, for he is your lord.
¹²The princes of Tyre* will shower you with
gifts.
People of great wealth will entreat your favor.

¹³The bride, a princess, waits within her
chamber,
dressed in a gown woven with gold.
¹⁴In her beautiful robes, she is led to the king,
accompanied by her bridesmaids.
¹⁵What a joyful, enthusiastic procession
as they enter the king's palace!

¹⁶Your sons will become kings like their father.
You will make them rulers over many lands.

¹⁷I will bring honor to your name in every
generation.
Therefore, the nations will praise you forever
and ever.

## PSALM 46

*For the choir director: A psalm of the descendants
of Korah, to be sung by soprano voices.* A song.*

¹God is our refuge and strength,
always ready to help in times of trouble.
²So we will not fear, even if earthquakes come
and the mountains crumble into the sea.
³Let the oceans roar and foam.
Let the mountains tremble as the waters surge!
*Interlude*

PSALM 42:1-2   As an artist I respond especially
to the passion exhibited in the psalms. Our spirit's cry
for fulfillment is as desperate as our physical need for
water. The word *thirst* suggested to me using a pointil-
listic technique. I used lighter dots of color for addi-
tional spray around the letters to create a sense of the
words emerging from the art.

⁴A river brings joy to the city of our God,
the sacred home of the Most High.
⁵God himself lives in that city; it cannot be
destroyed.
God will protect it at the break of day.
⁶The nations are in an uproar,
and kingdoms crumble!
God thunders,
and the earth melts!

⁷The LORD Almighty is here among us;
the God of Israel* is our fortress.   *Interlude*

**45:12** Hebrew *The daughter of Tyre.* **46:TITLE** Hebrew *according to alamoth.* **46:7** Hebrew *of Jacob;* also in 46:11.

⁸Come, see the glorious works of the LORD:
  See how he brings destruction upon the world
⁹and causes wars to end throughout the earth.
  He breaks the bow and snaps the spear
    in two;
  he burns the shields with fire.

¹⁰"Be silent, and know that I am God!
  I will be honored by every nation.
  I will be honored throughout the world."

¹¹The LORD Almighty is here among us;
  the God of Israel is our fortress.    *Interlude*

## PSALM 47

*For the choir director: A psalm of the descendants
of Korah.*

¹Come, everyone, and clap your hands for joy!
  Shout to God with joyful praise!
²For the LORD Most High is awesome.
  He is the great King of all the earth.
³He subdues the nations before us,
  putting our enemies beneath our feet.
⁴He chose the Promised Land as our inheritance,
  the proud possession of Jacob's descendants,
    whom he loves.    *Interlude*

⁵God has ascended with a mighty shout.
  The LORD has ascended with trumpets
    blaring.
⁶Sing praise to God, sing praises;
  sing praise to our King, sing praises!

⁷For God is the King over all the earth.
  Praise him with a psalm!
⁸God reigns above the nations,
  sitting on his holy throne.
⁹The rulers of the world have gathered together.
  They join us in praising the God of Abraham.
  For all the kings of the earth belong to God.
  He is highly honored everywhere.

## PSALM 48

*A psalm of the descendants of Korah. A song.*

¹How great is the LORD,
  and how much we should praise him

in the city of our God,
  which is on his holy mountain!
²It is magnificent in elevation—
  the whole earth rejoices to see it!
  Mount Zion, the holy mountain,*
    is the city of the great King!
³God himself is in Jerusalem's towers.
  He reveals himself as her defender.

⁴The kings of the earth joined forces
  and advanced against the city.
⁵But when they saw it, they were stunned;
  they were terrified and ran away.
⁶They were gripped with terror,
  like a woman writhing in the pain of
    childbirth
⁷or like the mighty ships of Tarshish
  being shattered by a powerful east wind.

⁸We had heard of the city's glory,
  but now we have seen it ourselves—
  the city of the LORD Almighty.
  It is the city of our God;
  he will make it safe forever.    *Interlude*

⁹O God, we meditate on your unfailing love
  as we worship in your Temple.
¹⁰As your name deserves, O God,
  you will be praised to the ends of the
    earth.
  Your strong right hand is filled with victory.
¹¹Let the people on Mount Zion rejoice.
  Let the towns of Judah be glad,
    for your judgments are just.

¹²Go, inspect the city of Jerusalem.*
  Walk around and count the many towers.
¹³Take note of the fortified walls,
  and tour all the citadels,

✎ PSALM 46:10-11   When I was growing up, my mother had a Pennsylvania Dutch expression for my inability to sit still: She would tell me not to act so "shushily." Now that I'm an adult, my tendency toward activity continues. Could this command possibly be more relevant to our stressful busyness today? Regarding the ornamentation of God's name, I've been challenged by the energy devoted in times past to such embellishment of the Scriptures.

48:2 Or *Mount Zion, in the far north*; Hebrew reads *Mount Zion, the heights of Zaphon.*  48:12 Hebrew *Zion.*

# BE SILENT
## AND
# KNOW
## THAT
# I AM

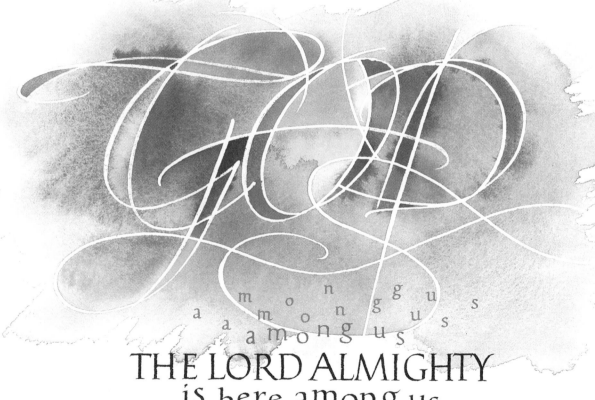

among us
among us
among us

**THE LORD ALMIGHTY**
is here among us
among us
among us

that you may describe them
    to future generations.
14For that is what God is like.
    He is our God forever and ever,
    and he will be our guide until we die.

## PSALM 49

*For the choir director: A psalm of the descendants of Korah.*

1Listen to this, all you people!
    Pay attention, everyone in the world!
2High and low,
    rich and poor—listen!
3For my words are wise,
    and my thoughts are filled with insight.
4I listen carefully to many proverbs
    and solve riddles with inspiration from
    a harp.

5There is no need to fear when times of trouble
    come,
    when enemies are surrounding me.
6They trust in their wealth
    and boast of great riches.
7Yet they cannot redeem themselves from death*
    by paying a ransom to God.
8Redemption does not come so easily,
    for no one can ever pay enough
9to live forever
    and never see the grave.

10Those who are wise must finally die,
    just like the foolish and senseless,
    leaving all their wealth behind.
11The grave is their eternal home,
    where they will stay forever.
    They may name their estates after themselves,
    but they leave their wealth to others.
12They will not last long despite their riches—
    they will die like the animals.
13This is the fate of fools,
    though they will be remembered as being
    so wise.   *Interlude*

14Like sheep, they are led to the grave,
    where death will be their shepherd.

In the morning the godly will rule over them.
    Their bodies will rot in the grave,
    far from their grand estates.
15But as for me, God will redeem my life.
    He will snatch me from the power of death.
    *Interlude*

16So don't be dismayed when the wicked
    grow rich,
    and their homes become ever more splendid.
17For when they die, they carry nothing with
    them.
    Their wealth will not follow them into
    the grave.
18In this life they consider themselves fortunate,
    and the world loudly applauds their success.
19But they will die like all others before them
    and never again see the light of day.
20People who boast of their wealth don't
    understand
    that they will die like the animals.

## PSALM 50

*A psalm of Asaph.*

1The mighty God, the LORD, has spoken;
    he has summoned all humanity from east to
    west!
2From Mount Zion, the perfection of beauty,
    God shines in glorious radiance.
3Our God approaches with the noise of thunder.
    Fire devours everything in his way,
    and a great storm rages around him.
4Heaven and earth will be his witnesses
    as he judges his people:
5"Bring my faithful people to me—
    those who made a covenant with me by
    giving sacrifices."

PSALM 47:1-2   Because I am a visually oriented person, the most powerful way for me to worship God is demonstratively—with my body. It requires more of myself. Clapping is for everyone, according to the psalmist, so it must be good for us. Our greatest enthusiasm should be reserved for the Lord. Such worship goes beyond words, which sometimes fail to capture his awesome nature.

49:7 *Or no one can redeem the life of another.*

COME
EVERYONE
AND CLAP
YOUR HANDS
FOR JOY
SHOUT TO GOD
WITH
JOYFUL PRAISE
FOR
THE LORD MOST HIGH IS
AWESOME
HE IS THE GREAT KING OF ALL THE EARTH

6 Then let the heavens proclaim his justice,
    for God himself will be the judge.
        *Interlude*

7 "O my people, listen as I speak.
    Here are my charges against you, O Israel:
    I am God, your God!
8 I have no complaint about your sacrifices
    or the burnt offerings you constantly bring
        to my altar.
9 But I want no more bulls from your barns;
    I want no more goats from your pens.
10 For all the animals of the forest are mine,
    and I own the cattle on a thousand hills.
11 Every bird of the mountains
    and all the animals of the field belong to me.
12 If I were hungry, I would not mention it
        to you,
    for all the world is mine and everything in it.
13 I don't need the bulls you sacrifice;
    I don't need the blood of goats.
14 What I want instead is your true thanks to God;
    I want you to fulfill your vows to the
        Most High.
15 Trust me in your times of trouble,
    and I will rescue you,
    and you will give me glory."

16 But God says to the wicked:
    "Recite my laws no longer,
    and don't pretend that you obey me.
17 For you refuse my discipline
    and treat my laws like trash.
18 When you see a thief, you help him,
    and you spend your time with adulterers.
19 Your mouths are filled with wickedness,
    and your tongues are full of lies.
20 You sit around and slander a brother—
    your own mother's son.
21 While you did all this, I remained silent,
    and you thought I didn't care.
    But now I will rebuke you,
    listing all my charges against you.
22 Repent, all of you who ignore me,
    or I will tear you apart,
    and no one will help you.

23 But giving thanks is a sacrifice that truly
        honors me.
    If you keep to my path,
    I will reveal to you the salvation of God."

## PSALM 51

*For the choir director: A psalm of David, regarding the time Nathan the prophet came to him after David had committed adultery with Bathsheba.*

1 Have mercy on me, O God,
    because of your unfailing love.
    Because of your great compassion,
    blot out the stain of my sins.
2 Wash me clean from my guilt.
    Purify me from my sin.

3 For I recognize my shameful deeds—
    they haunt me day and night.
4 Against you, and you alone, have I sinned;
    I have done what is evil in your sight.
    You will be proved right in what you say,
    and your judgment against me is just.

5 For I was born a sinner—
    yes, from the moment my mother
        conceived me.
6 But you desire honesty from the heart,
    so you can teach me to be wise in my
        inmost being.

7 Purify me from my sins,* and I will be
        clean;
    wash me, and I will be whiter than snow.
8 Oh, give me back my joy again;
    you have broken me—
    now let me rejoice.
9 Don't keep looking at my sins.
    Remove the stain of my guilt.
10 Create in me a clean heart, O God.
    Renew a right spirit within me.

PSALM 49:8-10, 15  Money doesn't have ultimate power. You can't buy eternal life. Wisdom also is inadequate to save our life from death. In both cases we see that people are ultimately equal. But the psalmist gives evidence of a hope beyond the grave, symbolized here by the butterfly.

51:7 Hebrew *Purify me with the hyssop branch.*

No one can ever pay enough
to live forever
and never see the grave.
Those who are wise
must finally die
just like the foolish and senseless,
leaving all their
wealth behind,

BUT AS FOR ME

God will redeem my life
He will snatch me
from the power of death

11 Do not banish me from your presence,
   and don't take your Holy Spirit from me.
12 Restore to me again the joy of your salvation,
   and make me willing to obey you.
13 Then I will teach your ways to sinners,
   and they will return to you.
14 Forgive me for shedding blood, O God who
      saves;
   then I will joyfully sing of your forgiveness.
15 Unseal my lips, O Lord,
   that I may praise you.

16 You would not be pleased with sacrifices,
   or I would bring them.
 If I brought you a burnt offering,
   you would not accept it.
17 The sacrifice you want is a broken spirit.
   A broken and repentant heart, O God,
   you will not despise.

18 Look with favor on Zion and help her;
   rebuild the walls of Jerusalem.
19 Then you will be pleased with worthy
      sacrifices
   and with our whole burnt offerings;
   and bulls will again be sacrificed on your altar.

## PSALM 52

*For the choir director: A psalm of David, regarding the time Doeg the Edomite told Saul that Ahimelech had given refuge to David.*

1 You call yourself a hero, do you?
   Why boast about this crime of yours,
   you who have disgraced God's people?
2 All day long you plot destruction.
   Your tongue cuts like a sharp razor;
   you're an expert at telling lies.
3 You love evil more than good
   and lies more than truth.        *Interlude*

4 You love to say things that harm others,
   you liar!
5 But God will strike you down once and
   for all.
   He will pull you from your home
   and drag you from the land of the living.
        *Interlude*

6 The righteous will see it and be amazed.
   They will laugh and say,
7 "Look what happens to mighty warriors
   who do not trust in God.
   They trust their wealth instead
   and grow more and more bold in their
      wickedness."

8 But I am like an olive tree,
   thriving in the house of God.
 I trust in God's unfailing love
   forever and ever.
9 I will praise you forever, O God,
   for what you have done.
 I will wait for your mercies
   in the presence of your people.

## PSALM 53

*For the choir director: A meditation of David.*

1 Only fools say in their hearts,
   "There is no God."
 They are corrupt, and their actions are
      evil;
   no one does good!

2 God looks down from heaven
   on the entire human race;
 he looks to see if there is even one with real
      understanding,
   one who seeks for God.
3 But no, all have turned away from God;
   all have become corrupt.
 No one does good,
   not even one!

4 Will those who do evil never learn?
   They eat up my people like bread;
   they wouldn't think of praying to God.
5 But then terror will grip them,
   terror like they have never known
      before.

✏ PSALM 51:4, 7, 10-12   To think that what I have done offends the almighty holy God! Yet he is willing to forgive. I can begin again. Snow is such a powerful image of purity. In a storm the whole landscape which may be marred with wreckage is transformed into a white blanket.

Against you,
and you alone,
have I sinned;
I have done
what is evil
in your sight

PURIFY ME FROM MY SINS
AND I WILL BE CLEAN
WASH ME AND I WILL BE
WHITER THAN SNOW

Create in me a clean heart, O God
Renew a right spirit within me
Do not banish me from your presence
and don't take your Holy Spirit from me
Restore to me again the joy of your salvation

God will scatter the bones of your enemies.
  You will put them to shame, for God has
    rejected them.

⁶Oh, that salvation would come from Mount
    Zion to rescue Israel!
  For when God restores his people,
  Jacob will shout with joy, and Israel will
    rejoice.

## PSALM 54

*For the choir director: A meditation of David, regarding the time the Ziphites came and said to Saul, "We know where David is hiding." To be accompanied by stringed instruments.*

¹Come with great power, O God, and rescue me!
  Defend me with your might.
²O God, listen to my prayer.
  Pay attention to my plea.

³For strangers are attacking me;
  violent men are trying to kill me.
  They care nothing for God.      *Interlude*

⁴But God is my helper.
  The Lord is the one who keeps me alive!
⁵May my enemies' plans for evil be turned
    against them.
  Do as you promised and put an end to them.

⁶I will sacrifice a voluntary offering to you;
  I will praise your name, O LORD, for it is good.
⁷For you will rescue me from my troubles
  and help me to triumph over my enemies.

## PSALM 55

*For the choir director: A psalm of David, to be accompanied by stringed instruments.*

¹Listen to my prayer, O God.
  Do not ignore my cry for help!
²Please listen and answer me,
  for I am overwhelmed by my troubles.
³My enemies shout at me,
  making loud and wicked threats.
  They bring trouble on me,
    hunting me down in their anger.

**55:15** Hebrew *let Sheol.*

⁴My heart is in anguish.
  The terror of death overpowers me.
⁵Fear and trembling overwhelm me.
  I can't stop shaking.
⁶Oh, how I wish I had wings like a dove;
  then I would fly away and rest!
⁷I would fly far away
  to the quiet of the wilderness.      *Interlude*

⁸How quickly I would escape—
  far away from this wild storm of hatred.

⁹Destroy them, Lord, and confuse their speech,
  for I see violence and strife in the city.
¹⁰Its walls are patrolled day and night against
    invaders,
  but the real danger is wickedness within the
    city.
¹¹Murder and robbery are everywhere there;
  threats and cheating are rampant in the streets.

¹²It is not an enemy who taunts me—
  I could bear that.
  It is not my foes who so arrogantly insult me—
    I could have hidden from them.
¹³Instead, it is you—my equal,
  my companion and close friend.
¹⁴What good fellowship we enjoyed
  as we walked together to the house of God.

¹⁵Let death seize my enemies by surprise;
  let the grave* swallow them alive,
  for evil makes its home within them.
¹⁶But I will call on God,
  and the LORD will rescue me.
¹⁷Morning, noon, and night
  I plead aloud in my distress,
  and the LORD hears my voice.
¹⁸He rescues me and keeps me safe
  from the battle waged against me,
  even though many still oppose me.

PSALM 53:1-3   The seriousness of this warning is underscored by its repetition from Psalm 14. For those of us who feel pretty good about ourselves, this is a serious attack—because God's perspective is far different from ours. So I decided to illustrate that distortion in our heart that keeps us from intimacy with God.

God looks down from heaven on the entire human race; he looks to see if there is even one with real understanding, one who seeks for God. But no, all have turned away from God; all have become corrupt. No one does good, not even one!

ONLY FOOLS SAY IN THEIR HEARTS "THERE IS NO GOD

19 God, who is king forever,
    will hear me and will humble them.
        *Interlude*
For my enemies refuse to change their ways;
    they do not fear God.

20 As for this friend of mine, he betrayed me;
    he broke his promises.
21 His words are as smooth as cream,
    but in his heart is war.
His words are as soothing as lotion,
    but underneath are daggers!

22 Give your burdens to the LORD,
    and he will take care of you.
He will not permit the godly to slip
    and fall.

23 But you, O God, will send the wicked
    down to the pit of destruction.
Murderers and liars will die young,
    but I am trusting you to save me.

## PSALM 56

*For the choir director: A psalm of David, regarding the time the Philistines seized him in Gath. To be sung to the tune "Dove on Distant Oaks."*

1 O God, have mercy on me.
    The enemy troops press in on me.
    My foes attack me all day long.
2 My slanderers hound me constantly,
    and many are boldly attacking me.
3 But when I am afraid,
    I put my trust in you.
4 O God, I praise your word.
    I trust in God, so why should I be afraid?
    What can mere mortals do to me?

5 They are always twisting what I say;
    they spend their days plotting ways to harm
        me.
6 They come together to spy on me—
    watching my every step, eager to kill me.
7 Don't let them get away with their
        wickedness;
    in your anger, O God, throw them to the
        ground.

8 You keep track of all my sorrows.
    You have collected all my tears in your
        bottle.
    You have recorded each one in your book.

9 On the very day I call to you for help,
    my enemies will retreat.
    This I know: God is on my side.★
10 O God, I praise your word.
    Yes, LORD, I praise your word.
11 I trust in God, so why should I be afraid?
    What can mere mortals do to me?

12 I will fulfill my vows to you, O God,
    and offer a sacrifice of thanks for your help.
13 For you have rescued me from death;
    you have kept my feet from slipping.
So now I can walk in your presence, O God,
    in your life-giving light.

## PSALM 57

*For the choir director: A psalm of David, regarding the time he fled from Saul and went into the cave. To be sung to the tune "Do Not Destroy!"*

1 Have mercy on me, O God, have mercy!
    I look to you for protection.
I will hide beneath the shadow of your wings
    until this violent storm is past.

2 I cry out to God Most High,
    to God who will fulfill his purpose for me.
3 He will send help from heaven to save me,
    rescuing me from those who are out to get
        me.    *Interlude*
My God will send forth his unfailing love and
    faithfulness.

4 I am surrounded by fierce lions
    who greedily devour human prey—
whose teeth pierce like spears and arrows,
    and whose tongues cut like swords.

✎ PSALM 55:6, 9-11  These words aren't real for those who don't live in urban settings, but the media reminds us. We always seem to need more police. Fear grows. A middle-class suburban lifestyle often means that we can "fly away" to escape, but there are no vacations for the poor.

56:9 Or *By this I will know that God is on my side.*

I see
violence and
strife in the city.
Its walks are
but the
real danger
is wickedness
within
the city,
patrolled
day and night
against invaders
murder and
robbery are
Oh, how I wish I had wings like a dove
then I would fly away and rest
everywhere there.
threats and cheating
are rampant in the streets.

5 Be exalted, O God, above the highest
    heavens!
  May your glory shine over all the earth.

6 My enemies have set a trap for me.
    I am weary from distress.
  They have dug a deep pit in my path,
    but they themselves have fallen into it.
        *Interlude*

7 My heart is confident in you, O God;
    no wonder I can sing your praises!
8 Wake up, my soul!
    Wake up, O harp and lyre!
    I will waken the dawn with my song.
9 I will thank you, Lord, in front of all the
    people.
    I will sing your praises among the nations.
10 For your unfailing love is as high as the
    heavens.
    Your faithfulness reaches to the clouds.

11 Be exalted, O God, above the highest
    heavens.
  May your glory shine over all the earth.

## PSALM 58

*For the choir director: A psalm of David, to be sung
to the tune "Do Not Destroy!"*

1 Justice—do you rulers know the meaning
    of the word?
    Do you judge the people fairly?
2 No, all your dealings are crooked;
    you hand out violence instead of justice.
3 These wicked people are born sinners;
    even from birth they have lied and gone
    their own way.
4 They spit poison like deadly snakes;
    they are like cobras that refuse to listen,
5 ignoring the tunes of the snake charmers,
    no matter how skillfully they play.

6 Break off their fangs, O God!
    Smash the jaws of these lions, O LORD!
7 May they disappear like water into thirsty
    ground.
    Make their weapons useless in their hands.*

8 May they be like snails that dissolve into slime,
    like a stillborn child who will never see
    the sun.
9 God will sweep them away, both young and old,
    faster than a pot heats on an open flame.

10 The godly will rejoice when they see injustice
    avenged.
    They will wash their feet in the blood of the
    wicked.
11 Then at last everyone will say,
    "There truly is a reward for those who live
    for God;
    surely there is a God who judges justly here
    on earth."

## PSALM 59

*For the choir director: A psalm of David, regarding the
time Saul sent soldiers to watch David's house in order
to kill him. To be sung to the tune "Do Not Destroy!"*

1 Rescue me from my enemies, O God.
    Protect me from those who have come
    to destroy me.
2 Rescue me from these criminals;
    save me from these murderers.

3 They have set an ambush for me.
    Fierce enemies are out there waiting,
    though I have done them no wrong,
    O LORD.
4 Despite my innocence, they prepare to kill me.
    Rise up and help me! Look on my plight!
5 O LORD God Almighty, the God of Israel,
    rise up to punish hostile nations.
    Show no mercy to wicked traitors.
        *Interlude*

6 They come at night,
    snarling like vicious dogs
    as they prowl the streets.
7 Listen to the filth that comes from their
    mouths,
    the piercing swords that fly from their lips.
    "Who can hurt us?" they sneer.

8 But LORD, you laugh at them.
    You scoff at all the hostile nations.

---

**58:7** Or *Let them be trodden down and wither like grass.* The meaning of the Hebrew is uncertain.

⁹You are my strength; I wait for you to
    rescue me,
        for you, O God, are my place of safety.
¹⁰In his unfailing love, my God will come and
    help me.
        He will let me look down in triumph on all
        my enemies.

¹¹Don't kill them, for my people soon forget
    such lessons;
        stagger them with your power, and bring
        them to their knees,
            O Lord our shield.
¹²Because of the sinful things they say,
        because of the evil that is on their lips,
    let them be captured by their pride,
        their curses, and their lies.
¹³Destroy them in your anger!
        Wipe them out completely!
    Then the whole world will know
        that God reigns in Israel.*     *Interlude*

¹⁴My enemies come out at night,
        snarling like vicious dogs
        as they prowl the streets.
¹⁵They scavenge for food
        but go to sleep unsatisfied.*

¹⁶But as for me, I will sing about your power.
        I will shout with joy each morning because
        of your unfailing love.
    For you have been my refuge,
        a place of safety in the day of distress.

¹⁷O my Strength, to you I sing praises,
        for you, O God, are my refuge,
        the God who shows me unfailing love.

## PSALM 60

*For the choir director: A psalm of David useful for teaching, regarding the time David fought Aram-naharaim and Aram-zobah, and Joab returned and killed twelve thousand Edomites in the Valley of Salt. To be sung to the tune "Lily of the Testimony."*

¹You have rejected us, O God, and broken our
    defenses.
        You have been angry with us; now restore us
        to your favor.

59:13 Hebrew *in Jacob.*  59:15 Or *and growl if they don't get enough.*

PSALM 56:8-9   I like the oriental pointed brush because it helps me make less controlled marks of raw emotion.  In contrast,  the smaller words form a path into an imaginary receptacle. This piece is reworked from my earlier book *Doorposts.* One of my most treasured letters came from a nurse in an AIDS clinic who shared that she has seen many tears shed over my expression of these words.

²You have shaken our land and split it
    open.
        Seal the cracks before it completely
        collapses.
³You have been very hard on us,
        making us drink wine that sent us reeling.

⁴But you have raised a banner for those who
    honor you—
        a rallying point in the face of attack.
            *Interlude*

⁵Use your strong right arm to save us,
    and rescue your beloved people.
⁶God has promised this by his holiness*:
    "I will divide up Shechem with joy.
    I will measure out the valley of Succoth.
⁷Gilead is mine,
    and Manasseh is mine.
  Ephraim will produce my warriors,
    and Judah will produce my kings.
⁸Moab will become my lowly servant,
    and Edom will be my slave.
    I will shout in triumph over the Philistines."

⁹But who will bring me into the fortified city?
    Who will bring me victory over Edom?
¹⁰Have you rejected us, O God?
    Will you no longer march with our armies?
¹¹Oh, please help us against our enemies,
    for all human help is useless.
¹²With God's help we will do mighty things,
    for he will trample down our foes.

## PSALM 61

*For the choir director: A psalm of David, to be accompanied by stringed instruments.*

¹O God, listen to my cry!
    Hear my prayer!
²From the ends of the earth,
    I will cry to you for help,
        for my heart is overwhelmed.
  Lead me to the towering rock of safety,
³    for you are my safe refuge,
        a fortress where my enemies cannot
            reach me.
⁴Let me live forever in your sanctuary,
    safe beneath the shelter of your wings!
        *Interlude*
⁵For you have heard my vows, O God.
    You have given me an inheritance reserved
        for those who fear your name.

**60:6** Or *in his sanctuary.*

⁶Add many years to the life of the king!
    May his years span the generations!
⁷May he reign under God's protection
    forever.
  Appoint your unfailing love and faithfulness
    to watch over him.

⁸Then I will always sing praises to your name
    as I fulfill my vows day after day.

## PSALM 62

*For Jeduthun, the choir director: A psalm of David.*

¹I wait quietly before God,
    for my salvation comes from him.
²He alone is my rock and my salvation,
    my fortress where I will never be shaken.

³So many enemies against one man—
    all of them trying to kill me.
  To them I'm just a broken-down wall
    or a tottering fence.
⁴They plan to topple me from my high
        position.
    They delight in telling lies about me.
  They are friendly to my face,
    but they curse me in their hearts.    *Interlude*

⁵I wait quietly before God,
    for my hope is in him.
⁶He alone is my rock and my salvation,
    my fortress where I will not be
        shaken.
⁷My salvation and my honor come from
        God alone.
  He is my refuge, a rock where no enemy
    can reach me.

⁸O my people, trust in him at all times.
    Pour out your heart to him,
        for God is our refuge.    *Interlude*

⁹From the greatest to the lowliest—
    all are nothing in his sight.
  If you weigh them on the scales,
    they are lighter than a puff of air.
¹⁰Don't try to get rich
    by extortion or robbery.

And if your wealth increases,
    don't make it the center of your life.

¹¹ God has spoken plainly,
    and I have heard it many times:
Power, O God, belongs to you;
¹²    unfailing love, O Lord, is yours.
Surely you judge all people
    according to what they have done.

## PSALM 63

*A psalm of David, regarding a time when David
was in the wilderness of Judah.*

¹ O God, you are my God;
    I earnestly search for you.
My soul thirsts for you;
    my whole body longs for you
in this parched and weary land
    where there is no water.

² I have seen you in your sanctuary
    and gazed upon your power and glory.
³ Your unfailing love is better to me than
        life itself;
    how I praise you!
⁴ I will honor you as long as I live,
    lifting up my hands to you in prayer.
⁵ You satisfy me more than the richest of foods.
    I will praise you with songs of joy.

⁶ I lie awake thinking of you,
    meditating on you through the night.
⁷ I think how much you have helped me;
    I sing for joy in the shadow of your
        protecting wings.
⁸ I follow close behind you;
    your strong right hand holds me securely.

⁹ But those plotting to destroy me will
        come to ruin.
    They will go down into the depths
        of the earth.
¹⁰ They will die by the sword
    and become the food of jackals.

¹¹ But the king will rejoice in God.
    All who trust in him will praise him,
    while liars will be silenced.

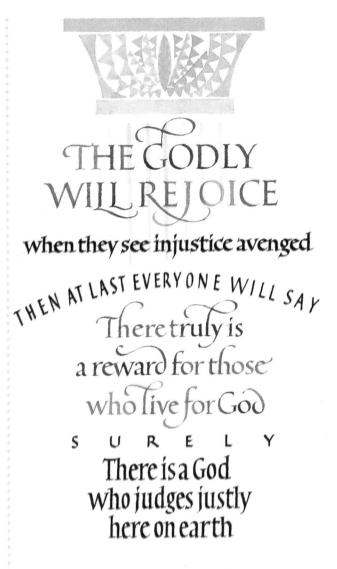

THE GODLY
WILL REJOICE

when they see injustice avenged

THEN AT LAST EVERYONE WILL SAY
There truly is
a reward for those
who live for God
S U R E L Y
There is a God
who judges justly
here on earth

PSALM 58:10-11   Sometimes the upright are
made fun of for their moral stand.  Our culture doesn't
really believe in a future judgment by God. This unique
capital is from a column I found in a book on synagogue
architecture. To me it represents the stature of one who
models for others the less convenient way of justice.

## PSALM 64

*For the choir director: A psalm of David.*

¹ O God, listen to my complaint.
    Do not let my enemies' threats overwhelm me.
² Protect me from the plots of the wicked,
    from the scheming of those who do evil.
³ Sharp tongues are the swords they wield;
    bitter words are the arrows they aim.

⁴They shoot from ambush at the innocent,
  attacking suddenly and fearlessly.
⁵They encourage each other to do evil
  and plan how to set their traps.
  "Who will ever notice?" they ask.
⁶As they plot their crimes, they say,
  "We have devised the perfect plan!"
  Yes, the human heart and mind are
    cunning.

⁷But God himself will shoot them down.
  Suddenly, his arrows will pierce them.
⁸Their own words will be turned against
    them, destroying them.
  All who see it happening will shake their
    heads in scorn.
⁹Then everyone will stand in awe,
  proclaiming the mighty acts of God,
  realizing all the amazing things he does.

¹⁰The godly will rejoice in the LORD
  and find shelter in him.
  And those who do what is right
  will praise him.

## PSALM 65

*For the choir director: A psalm of David. A song.*

¹What mighty praise, O God,
  belongs to you in Zion.
  We will fulfill our vows to you,
² for you answer our prayers,
  and to you all people will come.
³Though our hearts are filled with sins,
  you forgive them all.
⁴What joy for those you choose to bring
    near,
  those who live in your holy courts.
  What joys await us
  inside your holy Temple.

⁵You faithfully answer our prayers with
    awesome deeds,
  O God our savior.
  You are the hope of everyone on earth,
  even those who sail on distant seas.
⁶You formed the mountains by your power
  and armed yourself with mighty strength.

⁷You quieted the raging oceans
  with their pounding waves
  and silenced the shouting of the nations.
⁸Those who live at the ends of the earth
  stand in awe of your wonders.
  From where the sun rises to where it sets,
  you inspire shouts of joy.

⁹You take care of the earth and water it,
  making it rich and fertile.
  The rivers of God will not run dry;
  they provide a bountiful harvest of grain,
  for you have ordered it so.
¹⁰You drench the plowed ground with rain,
  melting the clods and leveling the ridges.
  You soften the earth with showers
  and bless its abundant crops.
¹¹You crown the year with a bountiful
    harvest;
  even the hard pathways overflow with
    abundance.
¹²The wilderness becomes a lush pasture,
  and the hillsides blossom with joy.
¹³The meadows are clothed with flocks of
    sheep,
  and the valleys are carpeted with grain.
  They all shout and sing for joy!

## PSALM 66

*For the choir director: A psalm. A song.*

¹Shout joyful praises to God, all the earth!
² Sing about the glory of his name!
  Tell the world how glorious he is.
³Say to God, "How awesome are your deeds!
  Your enemies cringe before your mighty
    power.
⁴Everything on earth will worship you;
  they will sing your praises,
  shouting your name in glorious songs."
    *Interlude*

PSALM 62:8-12  When we see the power struggles
that are common at home, at work, in sports, and in
the media, it becomes clear that we need a standard.
God displays the perfect balance of love and power. I
chose the shield as a symbol of our life and faith in him
as our refuge.

O MY PEOPLE
trust in him at all times
pour out your heart to him
FOR
GOD IS
OUR REFUGE
FROM THE GREATEST to the lowliest
all are nothing in his sight
IF YOU WEIGH THEM ON THE SCALES
they are lighter than a puff of air

Don't try to get rich
by extortion or robbery
AND if your wealth increases

DON'T MAKE IT THE CENTER OF YOUR LIFE

GOD has spoken plainly
many times
and I have heard it many times
many times

Power, O God, belongs to you;
unfailing love, O Lord, is yours
Surely, you judge all people
according to what they have done

5 Come and see what our God has done,
   what awesome miracles he does for his
      people!
6 He made a dry path through the Red Sea,*
   and his people went across on foot.
   Come, let us rejoice in who he is.
7 For by his great power he rules forever.
   He watches every movement of the nations;
   let no rebel rise in defiance.      *Interlude*

8 Let the whole world bless our God
   and sing aloud his praises.
9 Our lives are in his hands,
   and he keeps our feet from stumbling.
10 You have tested us, O God;
   you have purified us like silver melted
      in a crucible.
11 You captured us in your net
   and laid the burden of slavery on our backs.
12 You sent troops to ride across our broken
      bodies.
   We went through fire and flood.
   But you brought us to a place of great
      abundance.

13 Now I come to your Temple with burnt
      offerings
   to fulfill the vows I made to you—
14 yes, the sacred vows you heard me make
   when I was in deep trouble.
15 That is why I am sacrificing burnt offerings
      to you—
   the best of my rams as a pleasing aroma.
   And I will sacrifice bulls and goats.      *Interlude*

16 Come and listen, all you who fear God,
   and I will tell you what he did for me.
17 For I cried out to him for help,
   praising him as I spoke.
18 If I had not confessed the sin in my heart,
   my Lord would not have listened.
19 But God did listen!
   He paid attention to my prayer.

20 Praise God, who did not ignore my prayer
   and did not withdraw his unfailing love
      from me.

**66:6** Hebrew *the sea.*

## PSALM 67

*For the choir director: A psalm, to be accompanied
by stringed instruments. A song.*

1 May God be merciful and bless us.
   May his face shine with favor upon us.
      *Interlude*
2 May your ways be known throughout the
      earth,
   your saving power among people every-
      where.
3 May the nations praise you, O God.
   Yes, may all the nations praise you.

4 How glad the nations will be, singing for joy,
   because you govern them with justice
   and direct the actions of the whole world.
      *Interlude*
5 May the nations praise you, O God.
   Yes, may all the nations praise you.

6 Then the earth will yield its harvests,
   and God, our God, will richly bless us.
7 Yes, God will bless us,
   and people all over the world will fear him.

## PSALM 68

*For the choir director: A psalm of David. A song.*

1 Arise, O God, and scatter your enemies.
   Let those who hate God run for their lives.
2 Drive them off like smoke blown by the wind.
   Melt them like wax in fire.
   Let the wicked perish in the presence
      of God.
3 But let the godly rejoice.
   Let them be glad in God's presence.
   Let them be filled with joy.

4 Sing praises to God and to his name!
   Sing loud praises to him who rides the clouds.

PSALM 63:4-5 Flourishes (referred to as curlicues by people less familiar with calligraphy) are added to the ends of letters. Conceptually they are rooted in God's glory and his praise. The psalms encourage us to worship him with our mouth, our hands, our feet, and on our knees. Regardless of our posture, our heart must always be involved.

I will honor you
as long as I live
lifting up my hands
to you in prayer

You satisfy me
more than
the richest of foods
I will praise you
with songs of joy

His name is the LORD—
  rejoice in his presence!

5 Father to the fatherless, defender of widows—
  this is God, whose dwelling is holy.
6 God places the lonely in families;
  he sets the prisoners free and gives them joy.
  But for rebels, there is only famine and
    distress.

7 O God, when you led your people from Egypt,
  when you marched through the wilderness,
    *Interlude*
8 the earth trembled, and the heavens
    poured rain
  before you, the God of Sinai,
  before God, the God of Israel.
9 You sent abundant rain, O God,
  to refresh the weary Promised Land.
10 There your people finally settled,
  and with a bountiful harvest, O God,
  you provided for your needy people.

11 The Lord announces victory,
  and throngs of women shout the happy
    news.
12 Enemy kings and their armies flee,
  while the women of Israel divide the
    plunder.
13 Though they lived among the sheepfolds,
  now they are covered with silver and gold,
  as a dove is covered by its wings.
14 The Almighty scattered the enemy kings
  like a blowing snowstorm on Mount Zalmon.

15 The majestic mountains of Bashan
  stretch high into the sky.
16 Why do you look with envy, O rugged
    mountains,
  at Mount Zion, where God has chosen
    to live,
  where the LORD himself will live forever?

17 Surrounded by unnumbered thousands of
    chariots,
  the Lord came from Mount Sinai into his
    sanctuary.
18 When you ascended to the heights,
  you led a crowd of captives.

You received gifts from the people,
  even from those who rebelled against you.
  Now the LORD God will live among
    us here.

19 Praise the Lord; praise God our savior!
  For each day he carries us in his arms.
    *Interlude*
20 Our God is a God who saves!
  The Sovereign LORD rescues us from death.

21 But God will smash the heads of his enemies,
  crushing the skulls of those who love their
    guilty ways.
22 The Lord says, "I will bring my enemies down
    from Bashan;
  I will bring them up from the depths
    of the sea.
23 You, my people, will wash your feet in their
    blood,
  and even your dogs will get their share!"

24 Your procession has come into view,
    O God—
  the procession of my God and King
  as he goes into the sanctuary.
25 Singers are in front, musicians are behind;
  with them are young women playing
    tambourines.
26 Praise God, all you people of Israel;
  praise the LORD, the source of Israel's life.
27 Look, the little tribe of Benjamin leads the
    way.
  Then comes a great throng of rulers from
    Judah
  and all the rulers of Zebulun and Naphtali.

28 Summon your might, O God.
  Display your power, O God, as you have
    in the past.
29 The kings of the earth are bringing tribute
  to your Temple in Jerusalem.

✎ PSALM 65:5, 11-13 I have fond memories of
bountiful harvests: gathering eggs from five thousand
chickens, picking wild blueberries at Acadia National
Park, and witnessing the cherry blossoms in Tokyo. But
how will everyone on earth experience this abundance
unless we share?

YOU ARE THE HOPE OF

You crown the year with a bountiful harvest
The wilderness becomes a lush pasture
and the hillsides blossom with joy
The meadows are clothed with flocks of sheep
and the valleys are carpeted with grain
They all shout and sing for joy

EVERYONE ON EARTH

30 Rebuke these enemy nations—
   these wild animals lurking in the reeds,
   this herd of bulls among the weaker calves.
   Humble those who demand tribute from us.*
   Scatter the nations that delight in war.
31 Let Egypt come with gifts of precious metals;
   let Ethiopia* bow in submission to God.
32 Sing to God, you kingdoms of the earth.
   Sing praises to the Lord.        *Interlude*

33 Sing to the one who rides across the ancient
      heavens,
   his mighty voice thundering from the sky.
34 Tell everyone about God's power.
   His majesty shines down on Israel;
   his strength is mighty in the heavens.
35 God is awesome in his sanctuary.
   The God of Israel gives power and strength
      to his people.

   Praise be to God!

## PSALM 69

*For the choir director: A psalm of David, to be sung
to the tune "Lilies."*

1 Save me, O God,
   for the floodwaters are up to my neck.
2 Deeper and deeper I sink into the mire;
   I can't find a foothold to stand on.
   I am in deep water,
   and the floods overwhelm me.
3 I am exhausted from crying for help;
   my throat is parched and dry.
   My eyes are swollen with weeping,
   waiting for my God to help me.

4 Those who hate me without cause
   are more numerous than the hairs on my
      head.
   These enemies who seek to destroy me
   are doing so without cause.
   They attack me with lies,
   demanding that I give back what I didn't steal.

5 O God, you know how foolish I am;
   my sins cannot be hidden from you.

6 Don't let those who trust in you stumble
   because of me,
   O Sovereign LORD Almighty.
   Don't let me cause them to be humiliated,
   O God of Israel.
7 For I am mocked and shamed for your sake;
   humiliation is written all over my face.
8 Even my own brothers pretend they don't
      know me;
   they treat me like a stranger.

9 Passion for your house burns within me,
   so those who insult you are also insulting me.
10 When I weep and fast before the LORD,
   they scoff at me.
11 When I dress in sackcloth to show sorrow,
   they make fun of me.
12 I am the favorite topic of town gossip,
   and all the drunkards sing about me.

13 But I keep right on praying to you, LORD,
   hoping this is the time you will show
      me favor.
   In your unfailing love, O God,
   answer my prayer with your sure salvation.
14 Pull me out of the mud;
   don't let me sink any deeper!
   Rescue me from those who hate me,
   and pull me from these deep waters.
15 Don't let the floods overwhelm me,
   or the deep waters swallow me,
   or the pit of death devour me.

16 Answer my prayers, O LORD,
   for your unfailing love is wonderful.
   Turn and take care of me,
   for your mercy is so plentiful.
17 Don't hide from your servant;
   answer me quickly, for I am in deep trouble!

PSALM 67:2-4   What a wonderful community
the nations of the world would be if God's laws were
followed! But this requires that we be rescued from the
power of darkness. Even though God revealed himself
through the Hebrew people, it is his desire to be known
by all peoples. This is a time of great opportunity because
the spread of God's message has been accelerated
through air travel and telecommunications.

68:30 Or *Humble them until they submit, bringing pieces of silver as tribute.*   68:31 Hebrew *Cush.*

MAY YOUR WAYS BE KNOWN
THROUGHOUT THE EARTH
YOUR SAVING POWER
AMONG PEOPLE EVERYWHERE

MAY THE NATIONS PRAISE YOU, O GOD
YES, MAY ALL THE NATIONS PRAISE YOU
HOW GLAD THE NATIONS WILL BE
SINGING FOR JOY

BECAUSE YOU GOVERN THEM WITH JUSTICE
AND DIRECT THE ACTIONS
OF THE WHOLE WORLD

18 Come and rescue me;
    free me from all my enemies.

19 You know the insults I endure—
    the humiliation and disgrace.
  You have seen all my enemies
    and know what they have said.
20 Their insults have broken my heart,
    and I am in despair.
  If only one person would show some pity;
    if only one would turn and comfort me.
21 But instead, they give me poison for food;
    they offer me sour wine to satisfy my thirst.

22 Let the bountiful table set before them become
      a snare,
    and let their security become a trap.
23 Let their eyes go blind so they cannot see,
    and let their bodies grow weaker and weaker.
24 Pour out your fury on them;
    consume them with your burning anger.
25 May their homes become desolate
    and their tents be deserted.
26 To those you have punished, they add insult to
      injury;
    they scoff at the pain of those you have hurt.
27 Pile their sins up high,
    and don't let them go free.
28 Erase their names from the Book of Life;
    don't let them be counted among the
      righteous.

29 I am suffering and in pain.
    Rescue me, O God, by your saving power.

30 Then I will praise God's name with singing,
    and I will honor him with thanksgiving.
31 For this will please the LORD more than
      sacrificing an ox
    or presenting a bull with its horns and
      hooves.
32 The humble will see their God at work and
      be glad.
    Let all who seek God's help live in joy.
33 For the LORD hears the cries of his needy ones;
    he does not despise his people who are
      oppressed.

34 Praise him, O heaven and earth,
    the seas and all that move in them.
35 For God will save Jerusalem*
    and rebuild the towns of Judah.
  His people will live there
    and take possession of the land.
36 The descendants of those who obey him
      will inherit the land,
    and those who love him will live there in
      safety.

## PSALM 70

*For the choir director: A psalm of David, to bring us
to the LORD's remembrance.*

1 Please, God, rescue me!
    Come quickly, LORD, and help me.
2 May those who try to destroy me
    be humiliated and put to shame.
  May those who take delight in my trouble
    be turned back in disgrace.
3 Let them be horrified by their shame,
    for they said, "Aha! We've got him
      now!"
4 But may all who search for you
    be filled with joy and gladness.
  May those who love your salvation
    repeatedly shout, "God is great!"
5 But I am poor and needy;
    please hurry to my aid, O God.
  You are my helper and my savior;
    O LORD, do not delay!

## PSALM 71

1 O LORD, you are my refuge;
    never let me be disgraced.
2 Rescue me! Save me from my enemies,
    for you are just.
  Turn your ear to listen and set me free.

PSALM 68:5-6, 19   A brightly patterned quilt
invites us to be warmed even as our heavenly Father
warms us. He is a haven, God of the underdog; to be
with him is to be safe. I have a pen pal who is in prison.
He is an amazing example of the truth of this verse: He
has experienced God's forgiveness and enthusiastically
shares that freedom with fellow inmates.

**69:35** Hebrew *Zion.*

FATHER
TO THE
FATHERLESS
DEFENDER
of widows
THIS IS GOD
WHOSE DWELLING IS
H · O · L · Y
God places the lonely in families
HE SETS THE PRISONERS FREE
and gives them joy

PRAISE GOD
OUR SAVIOR
for each day
he carries us
in his arms

³Be to me a protecting rock of safety,
  where I am always welcome.
 Give the order to save me,
  for you are my rock and my fortress.

⁴My God, rescue me from the power of the
   wicked,
  from the clutches of cruel oppressors.
⁵O Lord, you alone are my hope.
  I've trusted you, O LORD, from childhood.
⁶Yes, you have been with me from birth;
  from my mother's womb you have cared for
   me.
 No wonder I am always praising you!

⁷My life is an example to many,
  because you have been my strength and
   protection.
⁸That is why I can never stop praising you;
  I declare your glory all day long.

⁹And now, in my old age, don't set me aside.
  Don't abandon me when my strength is
   failing.
¹⁰For my enemies are whispering against me.
  They are plotting together to kill me.
¹¹They say, "God has abandoned him.
  Let's go and get him,
  for there is no one to help him now."

¹²O God, don't stay away.
  My God, please hurry to help me.
¹³Bring disgrace and destruction on those who
   accuse me.
  May humiliation and shame cover
  those who want to harm me.

¹⁴But I will keep on hoping for you to help me;
  I will praise you more and more.
¹⁵I will tell everyone about your righteousness.
  All day long I will proclaim your saving
   power,
  for I am overwhelmed by how much you
   have done for me.
¹⁶I will praise your mighty deeds, O Sovereign
   LORD.
  I will tell everyone that you alone are just
   and good.

¹⁷O God, you have taught me from my earliest
   childhood,
  and I have constantly told others about the
   wonderful things you do.
¹⁸Now that I am old and gray,
  do not abandon me, O God.
 Let me proclaim your power to this new
   generation,
  your mighty miracles to all who come
   after me.

¹⁹Your righteousness, O God, reaches to the
   highest heavens.
  You have done such wonderful things.
  Who can compare with you, O God?
²⁰You have allowed me to suffer much
   hardship,
  but you will restore me to life again
  and lift me up from the depths of the
   earth.
²¹You will restore me to even greater honor
  and comfort me once again.

²²Then I will praise you with music on the
   harp,
  because you are faithful to your promises,
   O God.
 I will sing for you with a lyre,
  O Holy One of Israel.
²³I will shout for joy and sing your praises,
  for you have redeemed me.
²⁴I will tell about your righteous deeds
  all day long,
  for everyone who tried to hurt me
  has been shamed and humiliated.

## PSALM 72

*A psalm of Solomon.*

¹Give justice to the king, O God,
  and righteousness to the king's son.
²Help him judge your people in the right
   way;
  let the poor always be treated fairly.
³May the mountains yield prosperity for all,
  and may the hills be fruitful,
  because the king does what is right.

⁴Help him to defend the poor,
  to rescue the children of the needy,
  and to crush their oppressors.
⁵May he live* as long as the sun shines,
  as long as the moon continues in the skies.
  Yes, forever!
⁶May his reign be as refreshing as the spring-
    time rains—
  like the showers that water the earth.
⁷May all the godly flourish during his reign.
  May there be abundant prosperity until the
    end of time.

⁸May he reign from sea to sea,
  and from the Euphrates River* to the ends
    of the earth.
⁹Desert nomads will bow before him;
  his enemies will fall before him in the dust.
¹⁰The western kings of Tarshish and the islands
  will bring him tribute.
  The eastern kings of Sheba and Seba
  will bring him gifts.
¹¹All kings will bow before him,
  and all nations will serve him.

¹²He will rescue the poor when they cry
    to him;
  he will help the oppressed, who have no
    one to defend them.
¹³He feels pity for the weak and the needy,
  and he will rescue them.
¹⁴He will save them from oppression and from
    violence,
  for their lives are precious to him.

¹⁵Long live the king!
  May the gold of Sheba be given to him.
  May the people always pray for him
  and bless him all day long.
¹⁶May there be abundant crops throughout the
    land,
  flourishing even on the mountaintops.
  May the fruit trees flourish as they do in
    Lebanon,
  sprouting up like grass in a field.
¹⁷May the king's name endure forever;
  may it continue as long as the sun shines.

The humble WILL SEE THEIR GOD AT WORK and BE GLAD Let all who seek God's help live in joy

✒ PSALM 69:32   If we realize our need for God, he will respond to help us. The joy comes in the knowledge that he does care for us. As illustrated in the fable of the tortoise and the hare, our own natural abilities are not sufficient to win the race.

  May all nations be blessed through him
  and bring him praise.

¹⁸Bless the LORD God, the God of Israel,
  who alone does such wonderful things.
¹⁹Bless his glorious name forever!
  Let the whole earth be filled with his glory.
  Amen and amen!

²⁰(This ends the prayers of David son of Jesse.)

72:5 As in Greek version; Hebrew reads *May they fear you.*   72:8 Hebrew *the river.*

BOOK THREE (Psalms 73–89)

## PSALM 73

*A psalm of Asaph.*

¹ Truly God is good to Israel,
  to those whose hearts are pure.

² But as for me, I came so close to the edge
    of the cliff!
  My feet were slipping, and I was almost gone.
³ For I envied the proud
  when I saw them prosper despite their
    wickedness.
⁴ They seem to live such a painless life;
  their bodies are so healthy and strong.
⁵ They aren't troubled like other people
  or plagued with problems like everyone
    else.
⁶ They wear pride like a jeweled necklace,
  and their clothing is woven of cruelty.
⁷ These fat cats have everything
  their hearts could ever wish for!
⁸ They scoff and speak only evil;
  in their pride they seek to crush others.
⁹ They boast against the very heavens,
  and their words strut throughout the earth.
¹⁰ And so the people are dismayed and confused,
  drinking in all their words.
¹¹ "Does God realize what is going on?" they
    ask.
  "Is the Most High even aware of what is
    happening?"
¹² Look at these arrogant people—
  enjoying a life of ease while their riches
    multiply.

¹³ Was it for nothing that I kept my heart pure
  and kept myself from doing wrong?
¹⁴ All I get is trouble all
    day long;
  every morning brings me pain.

¹⁵ If I had really spoken this way,
  I would have been a traitor
    to your people.
¹⁶ So I tried to understand why
  the wicked prosper.
  But what a difficult task it is!

¹⁷ Then one day I went into your sanctuary,
    O God,
  and I thought about the destiny of the
    wicked.
¹⁸ Truly, you put them on a slippery path
  and send them sliding over the cliff to
    destruction.
¹⁹ In an instant they are destroyed,
  swept away by terrors.
²⁰ Their present life is only a dream
  that is gone when they awake.
  When you arise, O Lord,
  you will make them vanish from this life.

²¹ Then I realized how bitter I had become,
  how pained I had been by all I had seen.
²² I was so foolish and ignorant—
  I must have seemed like a senseless animal
    to you.
²³ Yet I still belong to you;
  you are holding my right hand.
²⁴ You will keep on guiding me with your
    counsel,
  leading me to a glorious destiny.
²⁵ Whom have I in heaven but you?
  I desire you more than anything on
    earth.
²⁶ My health may fail, and my spirit may
    grow weak,
  but God remains the strength of my heart;
  he is mine forever.

²⁷ But those who desert him will perish,
  for you destroy those who abandon you.
²⁸ But as for me, how good it is to be near
    God!
  I have made the Sovereign LORD my
    shelter,
  and I will tell everyone about the wonderful
    things you do.

🖋 PSALM 73:2-4, 6-7, 12-15   The lightning in this design represents the double dangers mentioned in the text. Those who live in luxury may forget God, and the poor who envy them may destroy themselves. As in caricature, these letters' proportions are exaggerated to bring out the drama of the text.

I came so close to the edge of the cliff
My feet were slipping, and I was almost gone
For I envied the proud
when I saw them prosper despite their wickedness

They seem to live such a painless life
their bodies are so healthy and strong
They wear pride like a jeweled necklace
and their clothing is woven of cruelty.
These fat cats have everything their hearts could ever wish for
Look at these arrogant people
enjoying a life of ease
while their riches multiply multiply
multiply

If I had
really spoken
this way,
I would
have been
a traitor
to your
people.

Was it for nothing that I kept my heart pure
and kept myself from doing wrong?
All I get is    trouble
trouble all day long
troubletrouble
Every morning brings me pain

## PSALM 74

*A psalm of Asaph.*

¹O God, why have you rejected us forever?
  Why is your anger so intense against the
    sheep of your own pasture?
²Remember that we are the people you chose
    in ancient times,
  the tribe you redeemed as your own special
    possession!
  And remember Jerusalem,★ your home here
    on earth.
³Walk through the awful ruins of the city;
  see how the enemy has destroyed your
    sanctuary.
⁴There your enemies shouted their victorious
    battle cries;
  there they set up their battle standards.
⁵They chopped down the entrance
  like woodcutters in a forest.
⁶With axes and picks,
  they smashed the carved paneling.
⁷They set the sanctuary on fire, burning it to
    the ground.
  They utterly defiled the place that bears
    your holy name.
⁸Then they thought, "Let's destroy every-
    thing!"
  So they burned down all the places where
    God was worshiped.

⁹We see no miraculous signs
  as evidence that you will save us.
  All the prophets are gone;
    no one can tell us when it will end.
¹⁰How long, O God, will you allow our
    enemies to mock you?
  Will you let them dishonor your name
    forever?
¹¹Why do you hold back your strong right
    hand?
  Unleash your powerful fist and deliver a
    deathblow.

¹²You, O God, are my king from ages past,
  bringing salvation to the earth.

¹³You split the sea by your strength
  and smashed the sea monster's heads.
¹⁴You crushed the heads of Leviathan
  and let the desert animals eat him.
¹⁵You caused the springs and streams to gush
    forth,
  and you dried up rivers that never run dry.
¹⁶Both day and night belong to you;
  you made the starlight★ and the sun.
¹⁷You set the boundaries of the earth,
  and you make both summer and winter.

¹⁸See how these enemies scoff at you, LORD.
  A foolish nation has dishonored your name.
¹⁹Don't let these wild beasts destroy your doves.
  Don't forget your afflicted people forever.

²⁰Remember your covenant promises,
  for the land is full of darkness and violence!
²¹Don't let the downtrodden be constantly
    disgraced!
  Instead, let these poor and needy ones give
    praise to your name.

²²Arise, O God, and defend your cause.
  Remember how these fools insult you all day
    long.
²³Don't overlook these things your enemies have
    said.
  Their uproar of rebellion grows ever louder.

## PSALM 75

*For the choir director: A psalm of Asaph, to be sung to the tune "Do Not Destroy!" A song.*

¹We thank you, O God!
  We give thanks because you are near.
  People everywhere tell of your mighty miracles.

²God says, "At the time I have planned,
  I will bring justice against the wicked.
³When the earth quakes and its people live
    in turmoil,
  I am the one who keeps its foundations firm.
    *Interlude*

⁴"I warned the proud, `Stop your boasting!'
  I told the wicked, `Don't raise your fists!

**74:2** Hebrew *Mount Zion.* **74:16** Or *moon;* Hebrew reads *light.*

⁵Don't lift your fists in defiance at the heavens
   or speak with rebellious arrogance.'"

⁶For no one on earth—from east or west,
   or even from the wilderness—
   can raise another person up.

⁷It is God alone who judges;
   he decides who will rise and who will fall.

⁸For the LORD holds a cup in his hand;
   it is full of foaming wine mixed with spices.
 He pours the wine out in judgment,
   and all the wicked must drink it,
   draining it to the dregs.

⁹But as for me, I will always proclaim what
     God has done;
   I will sing praises to the God of Israel.★

¹⁰For God says, "I will cut off the strength of the
     wicked,
   but I will increase the power of the godly."

## PSALM 76

*For the choir director: A psalm of Asaph, to be accompanied by stringed instruments. A song.*

¹God is well known in Judah;
   his name is great in Israel.
²Jerusalem★ is where he lives;
   Mount Zion is his home.
³There he breaks the arrows of the enemy,
   the shields and swords and weapons of his foes.
      *Interlude*

⁴You are glorious and more majestic
   than the everlasting mountains.★
⁵The mightiest of our enemies have been
     plundered.
   They lie before us in the sleep of death.
   No warrior could lift a hand against us.
⁶When you rebuked them, O God of Jacob,
   their horses and chariots stood still.

⁷No wonder you are greatly feared!
   Who can stand before you when your anger
     explodes?
⁸From heaven you sentenced your enemies;
   the earth trembled and stood silent before you.

WHOM HAVE I IN HEAVEN BUT YOU? I desire you more than anything on earth my health may fail and my spirit may grow weak BUT GOD REMAINS THE STRENGTH OF MY HEART He is mine forever

PSALM 73:25-26   Sometimes when people find out that I am a calligrapher they apologize for their own handwriting, admitting that they can't even write in a straight line. I always find this amusing because in much of my interpretive work I *choose* not to write in a straight line. In this design, everything but God swims on the page—to emphasize the stability he brings us.

⁹You stand up to judge those who do evil,
   O God,
   and to rescue the oppressed of the earth.
      *Interlude*

75:9 Hebrew *of Jacob.* 76:2 Hebrew *Salem,* another name for Jerusalem. 76:4 As in Greek version; Hebrew reads *than mountains filled with beasts of prey.*

10 Human opposition only enhances your glory,
　　for you use it as a sword of judgment.*

11 Make vows to the LORD your God, and fulfill
　　them.
　　Let everyone bring tribute to the Awesome
　　　One.

12 For he breaks the spirit of princes
　　and is feared by the kings of the earth.

## PSALM 77

*For Jeduthun, the choir director: A psalm of Asaph.*

1 I cry out to God without holding back.
　　Oh, that God would listen to me!

2 When I was in deep trouble,
　　I searched for the Lord.
　All night long I pray, with hands lifted toward
　　heaven, pleading.
　　There can be no joy for me until he acts.

3 I think of God, and I moan,
　　overwhelmed with longing for his help.
　　　*Interlude*

4 You don't let me sleep.
　　I am too distressed even to pray!

5 I think of the good old days, long since
　　ended,

6 　when my nights were filled with joyful songs.
　　I search my soul and think about the
　　　difference now.

7 Has the Lord rejected me forever?
　　Will he never again show me favor?

8 Is his unfailing love gone forever?
　　Have his promises permanently failed?

9 Has God forgotten to be kind?
　　Has he slammed the door on his compassion?
　　　*Interlude*

10 And I said, "This is my fate,
　　that the blessings of the Most High have
　　　changed to hatred."

11 I recall all you have done, O LORD;
　　I remember your wonderful deeds of
　　　long ago.

12 They are constantly in my thoughts.
　　I cannot stop thinking about them.

13 O God, your ways are holy.
　　Is there any god as mighty as you?

14 You are the God of miracles and wonders!
　　You demonstrate your awesome power
　　　among the nations.

15 You have redeemed your people by your
　　strength,
　　the descendants of Jacob and of Joseph
　　　by your might.　　*Interlude*

16 When the Red Sea* saw you, O God,
　　its waters looked and trembled!
　　The sea quaked to its very depths.

17 The clouds poured down their rain;
　　the thunder rolled and crackled in
　　　the sky.
　　Your arrows of lightning flashed.

18 Your thunder roared from the whirlwind;
　　the lightning lit up the world!
　　The earth trembled and shook.

19 Your road led through the sea,
　　your pathway through the mighty
　　　waters—
　　a pathway no one knew was there!

20 You led your people along that road like a
　　flock of sheep,
　　with Moses and Aaron as their shepherds.

## PSALM 78

*A psalm of Asaph.*

1 O my people, listen to my teaching.
　　Open your ears to what I am saying,

2 　for I will speak to you in a parable.
　I will teach you hidden lessons from our
　　　past—

3 　stories we have heard and know,
　　stories our ancestors handed down to us.

4 We will not hide these truths from our
　　children

✎ PSALM 75:2-3, 6-7　God is orchestrating the
ultimate drama in which he allows both good and
evil—but in which good will ultimately triumph. I
wanted to show both the earth quaking and God's
sovereign control, so I devised a kind of crown to
mimic the lines in the turmoil.

76:10 The meaning of the Hebrew is uncertain.　77:16 Hebrew *the waters.*

GOD SAYS
AT THE TIME I HAVE PLANNED
I WILL BRING JUSTICE AGAINST THE WICKED
when the earth quakes
and its people
live in turmoil

I AM THE ONE
WHO KEEPS ITS
FOUNDATIONS
FIRM
for no one on earth
from east or west
can raise another person up

IT IS GOD ALONE
WHO DECIDES WHO WILL RISE
and who will fall

but will tell the next generation about the
   glorious deeds of the LORD.
We will tell of his power and the mighty
   miracles he did.
5 For he issued his decree to Jacob;
   he gave his law to Israel.
He commanded our ancestors
   to teach them to their children,
6 so the next generation might know them—
   even the children not yet born—
   that they in turn might teach their children.
7 So each generation can set its hope anew
   on God,
   remembering his glorious miracles
   and obeying his commands.
8 Then they will not be like their ancestors—
   stubborn, rebellious, and unfaithful,
   refusing to give their hearts to God.

9 The warriors of Ephraim, though fully armed,
   turned their backs and fled when the day of
   battle came.
10 They did not keep God's covenant,
   and they refused to live by his law.
11 They forgot what he had done—
   the wonderful miracles he had shown them,
12   the miracles he did for their ancestors in
   Egypt, on the plain of Zoan.
13 For he divided the sea before them and led
   them through!
The water stood up like walls beside them!
14 In the daytime he led them by a cloud,
   and at night by a pillar of fire.
15 He split open the rocks in the wilderness
   to give them plenty of water, as from a
   gushing spring.
16 He made streams pour from the rock,
   making the waters flow down like a river!

17 Yet they kept on with their sin,
   rebelling against the Most High in the desert.
18 They willfully tested God in their hearts,
   demanding the foods they craved.
19 They even spoke against God himself, saying,
   "God can't give us food in the desert.
20 Yes, he can strike a rock so water gushes out,
   but he can't give his people bread and meat."

21 When the LORD heard them, he was angry.
   The fire of his wrath burned against Jacob.
Yes, his anger rose against Israel,
22   for they did not believe God
   or trust him to care for them.
23 But he commanded the skies to open—
   he opened the doors of heaven—
24   and rained down manna for them to eat.
He gave them bread from heaven.
25   They ate the food of angels!
God gave them all they could hold.
26 He released the east wind in the heavens
   and guided the south wind by his mighty
   power.
27 He rained down meat as thick as dust—
   birds as plentiful as the sands along the
   seashore!
28 He caused the birds to fall within their camp
   and all around their tents.
29 The people ate their fill.
   He gave them what they wanted.
30 But before they finished eating this food they
   had craved,
   while the meat was yet in their mouths,
31 the anger of God rose against them,
   and he killed their strongest men;
   he struck down the finest of Israel's young
   men.
32 But in spite of this, the people kept on sinning.
   They refused to believe in his miracles.
33 So he ended their lives in failure
   and gave them years of terror.

34 When God killed some of them, the rest finally
   sought him.
   They repented and turned to God.
35 Then they remembered that God was their rock,
   that their redeemer was the Most High.
36 But they followed him only with their words;
   they lied to him with their tongues.
37 Their hearts were not loyal to him.
   They did not keep his covenant.
38 Yet he was merciful and forgave their sins
   and didn't destroy them all.
Many a time he held back his anger
   and did not unleash his fury!

39 For he remembered that they were merely
      mortal,
   gone in a moment like a breath of wind,
      never to return.

40 Oh, how often they rebelled against him in the
      desert
   and grieved his heart in the wilderness.
41 Again and again they tested God's patience
   and frustrated the Holy One of Israel.
42 They forgot about his power
   and how he rescued them from their enemies.
43 They forgot his miraculous signs in Egypt,
   his wonders on the plain of Zoan.
44 For he turned their rivers into blood,
   so no one could drink from the streams.
45 He sent vast swarms of flies to consume them
   and hordes of frogs to ruin them.
46 He gave their crops to caterpillars;
   their harvest was consumed by locusts.
47 He destroyed their grapevines with hail
   and shattered their sycamores with sleet.
48 He abandoned their cattle to the hail,
   their livestock to bolts of lightning.
49 He loosed on them his fierce anger—
   all his fury, rage, and hostility.
   He dispatched against them
   a band of destroying angels.
50 He turned his anger against them;
   he did not spare the Egyptians' lives
   but handed them over to the plague.
51 He killed the oldest son in each Egyptian
      family,
   the flower of youth throughout the land
      of Egypt.*
52 But he led his own people like a flock of
      sheep,
   guiding them safely through the wilderness.
53 He kept them safe so they were not afraid;
   but the sea closed in upon their enemies.
54 He brought them to the border of his holy
      land,
   to this land of hills he had won for them.
55 He drove out the nations before them;
   he gave them their inheritance by lot.
   He settled the tribes of Israel into their homes.

78:51 Hebrew *in the tents of Ham.*

HE GAVE THEM BREAD FROM HEAVEN, THEY ATE THE FOOD OF ANGELS! GOD GAVE THEM ALL THEY COULD HOLD

PSALM 78:24-25   God supplied the early
Hebrews with food in a class by itself—meeting their
physical needs and symbolizing that which feeds our
souls as well. The delicate flourish represents that
spiritual dimension. This is an example where some
subtlety in the design is helpful because we don't know
exactly what manna looked like.

56 Yet though he did all this for them,
   they continued to test his patience.
   They rebelled against the Most High
   and refused to follow his decrees.
57 They turned back and were as faithless as their
      parents had been.
   They were as useless as a crooked bow.

58 They made God angry by building altars
to other gods;
they made him jealous with their idols.
59 When God heard them, he was very angry,
and he rejected Israel completely.
60 Then he abandoned his dwelling at Shiloh,
the Tabernacle where he had lived among
the people.
61 He allowed the Ark of his might to be
captured;
he surrendered his glory into enemy
hands.
62 He gave his people over to be butchered
by the sword,
because he was so angry with his own
people—his special possession.
63 Their young men were killed by fire;
their young women died before singing
their wedding songs.
64 Their priests were slaughtered,
and their widows could not mourn their
deaths.
65 Then the Lord rose up as though waking
from sleep,
like a mighty man aroused from a
drunken stupor.
66 He routed his enemies
and sent them to eternal shame.
67 But he rejected Joseph's descendants;
he did not choose the tribe of Ephraim.
68 He chose instead the tribe of Judah,
Mount Zion, which he loved.
69 There he built his towering sanctuary,
as solid and enduring as the earth
itself.
70 He chose his servant David,
calling him from the sheep pens.
71 He took David from tending the ewes and
lambs
and made him the shepherd of Jacob's
descendants—
God's own people, Israel.
72 He cared for them with a true heart
and led them with skillful hands.

**79:7** Hebrew *Jacob.*

## PSALM 79

*A psalm of Asaph.*

1 O God, pagan nations have conquered your
land, your special possession.
They have defiled your holy Temple
and made Jerusalem a heap of ruins.
2 They have left the bodies of your servants
as food for the birds of heaven.
The flesh of your godly ones
has become food for the wild animals.
3 Blood has flowed like water all around
Jerusalem;
no one is left to bury the dead.
4 We are mocked by our neighbors,
an object of scorn and derision to those
around us.

5 O LORD, how long will you be angry with us?
Forever?
How long will your jealousy burn like fire?
6 Pour out your wrath on the nations that refuse
to recognize you—
on kingdoms that do not call upon your name.
7 For they have devoured your people Israel,*
making the land a desolate wilderness.
8 Oh, do not hold us guilty for our former sins!
Let your tenderhearted mercies quickly meet
our needs,
for we are brought low to the dust.
9 Help us, O God of our salvation!
Help us for the honor of your name.
Oh, save us and forgive our sins
for the sake of your name.
10 Why should pagan nations be allowed to scoff,
asking, "Where is their God?"
Show us your vengeance against the nations,
for they have spilled the blood of your
servants.

PSALM 80:1, 7, 18 When we look at the perseverance of Israel, we see the hand of God. We can't study Psalms without recognizing his special care for her. There is a greater glory to God than what we have seen. I wanted to make a picture of some of that glory. Let us pray this psalm together, that God will bring more goodness into our culture.

Please listen, O Shepherd of Israel
you who lead Israel like a flock
God, enthroned above the cherubim
display your radiant glory

Turn us again to yourself
O God Almighty
Make your face shine down upon us
Only then will we be saved
Revive us so we can call on your name once more

P S A L M   8 0

11 Listen to the moaning of the prisoners.
   Demonstrate your great power by saving
      those condemned to die.

12 O Lord, take sevenfold vengeance on our
      neighbors
   for the scorn they have hurled at you.
13 Then we your people, the sheep of your pasture,
   will thank you forever and ever,
      praising your greatness from generation
         to generation.

## PSALM 80

*For the choir director: A psalm of Asaph, to be sung to*
*the tune "Lilies of the Covenant."*

1 Please listen, O Shepherd of Israel,
   you who lead Israel* like a flock.
 O God, enthroned above the cherubim,
   display your radiant glory
2   to Ephraim, Benjamin, and Manasseh.
 Show us your mighty power.
   Come to rescue us!

3 Turn us again to yourself, O God.
   Make your face shine down upon us.
   Only then will we be saved.

4 O LORD God Almighty,
   how long will you be angry and reject our
      prayers?
5 You have fed us with sorrow
   and made us drink tears by the bucketful.
6 You have made us the scorn of neighboring
      nations.
   Our enemies treat us as a joke.

7 Turn us again to yourself, O God Almighty.
   Make your face shine down upon us.
   Only then will we be saved.
8 You brought us from Egypt as though we
      were a tender vine;
   you drove away the pagan nations and
      transplanted us into your land.
9 You cleared the ground for us,
   and we took root and filled the land.
10 The mountains were covered with our
      shade;

the mighty cedars were covered with our
      branches.
11 We spread our branches west to the
      Mediterranean Sea,
   our limbs east to the Euphrates River.*
12 But now, why have you broken down our walls
   so that all who pass may steal our fruit?
13 The boar from the forest devours us,
   and the wild animals feed on us.

14 Come back, we beg you, O God Almighty.
   Look down from heaven and see our
      plight.
 Watch over and care for this vine
15   that you yourself have planted,
   this son you have raised for yourself.
16 For we are chopped up and burned by our
      enemies.
   May they perish at the sight of your frown.
17 Strengthen the man you love,
   the son of your choice.
18 Then we will never forsake you again.
   Revive us so we can call on your name
      once more.

19 Turn us again to yourself, O LORD God
      Almighty.
   Make your face shine down upon us.
   Only then will we be saved.

## PSALM 81

*For the choir director: A psalm of Asaph, to be accom-*
*panied by a stringed instrument.**

1 Sing praises to God, our strength.
   Sing to the God of Israel.*
2 Sing! Beat the tambourine.
   Play the sweet lyre and the harp.
3 Sound the trumpet for a sacred feast
   when the moon is new,
   when the moon is full.

PSALM 82:2-3   Three thousand years later,
injustice continues. Greed continues to drive people
in power. To illustrate this persistence of corruption,
I decided to imitate the passage of time on a clock.
Although the message of compassion is smaller, it
triumphs as light against the darkness.

80:1 Hebrew *Joseph.*  80:11 Hebrew *west to the sea, . . . east to the river.*  81:TITLE Hebrew *according to the gittith.*  81:1 Hebrew *of Jacob.*

How long
will you judges
hand down
unjust
decisions?

How long
will you shower
special favors
on the wicked?

GIVE FAIR
JUDGMENT
to the poor and the orphan

UPHOLD
THE RIGHTS
of the oppressed
and the destitute

⁴For this is required by the laws of Israel;
    it is a law of the God of Jacob.
⁵He made it a decree for Israel*
    when he attacked Egypt to set us free.

I heard an unknown voice that said,
⁶"Now I will relieve your shoulder of its
      burden;
    I will free your hands from their heavy
      tasks.
⁷You cried to me in trouble, and I saved you;
    I answered out of the thundercloud.
I tested your faith at Meribah,
    when you complained that there was no
      water.    *Interlude*

⁸"Listen to me, O my people, while I give
      you stern warnings.
    O Israel, if you would only listen!
⁹You must never have a foreign god;
    you must not bow down before a false
      god.
¹⁰For it was I, the LORD your God,
    who rescued you from the land of Egypt.
    Open your mouth wide, and I will fill it
      with good things.

¹¹"But no, my people wouldn't listen.
    Israel did not want me around.
¹²So I let them follow their blind and stubborn
      way,
    living according to their own desires.
¹³But oh, that my people would listen to me!
    Oh, that Israel would follow me, walking
      in my paths!
¹⁴How quickly I would then subdue their
      enemies!
    How soon my hands would be upon their
      foes!
¹⁵Those who hate the LORD would cringe
      before him;
    their desolation would last forever.
¹⁶But I would feed you with the best of
      foods.
    I would satisfy you with wild honey from
      the rock."

**81:5** Hebrew *for Joseph.*

## PSALM 82

*A psalm of Asaph.*

¹God presides over heaven's court;
    he pronounces judgment on the judges:
²"How long will you judges hand down unjust
      decisions?
    How long will you shower special favors on
      the wicked?    *Interlude*

³"Give fair judgment to the poor and the
      orphan;
    uphold the rights of the oppressed and the
      destitute.
⁴Rescue the poor and helpless;
    deliver them from the grasp of evil
      people.
⁵But these oppressors know nothing;
    they are so ignorant!
And because they are in darkness,
    the whole world is shaken to the core.
⁶I say, `You are gods
    and children of the Most High.
⁷But in death you are mere men.
    You will fall as any prince,
    for all must die.'"

⁸Rise up, O God, and judge the earth,
    for all the nations belong to you.

## PSALM 83

*A psalm of Asaph. A song.*

¹O God, don't sit idly by,
    silent and inactive!
²Don't you hear the tumult of your enemies?
    Don't you see what your arrogant enemies
      are doing?
³They devise crafty schemes against your people,
    laying plans against your precious ones.

✎ PSALM 84:1, 10  Seeing the magnificent architecture and decoration of Europe's cathedrals tells me that the people who built them had a vision of God's glory. We must not lose sight of God's character, which is the inspiration for the beauty. Otherwise the external charm becomes vain. Blessed are those who serve to build God's Kingdom rather than their own.

HOW
LOVELY
IS YOUR
DWELLING
PLACE
O LORD
ALMIGHTY

A SINGLE DAY
IN YOUR COURTS
IS BETTER THAN
a thousand anywhere else
a thousand anywhere else
thousand anywhere

I would rather be a gatekeeper in
THE HOUSE OF MY GOD
than live the good life
in the homes of the wicked

4 "Come," they say, "let us wipe out Israel as a
    nation.
    We will destroy the very memory of its
      existence."
5   This was their unanimous decision.
  They signed a treaty as allies against you—
6   these Edomites and Ishmaelites,
    Moabites and Hagrites,
7   Gebalites, Ammonites, and Amalekites,
    and people from Philistia and Tyre.
8 Assyria has joined them, too,
    and is allied with the descendants of Lot.
      *Interlude*

9 Do to them as you did to the Midianites
    or as you did to Sisera and Jabin at the
      Kishon River.
10 They were destroyed at Endor,
    and their decaying corpses fertilized the soil.
11 Let their mighty nobles die as Oreb and Zeeb
    did.
    Let all their princes die like Zebah and
      Zalmunna,
12 for they said, "Let us seize for our own use
    these pasturelands of God!"

13 O my God, blow them away like whirling dust,
    like chaff before the wind!
14 As a fire roars through a forest
    and as a flame sets mountains ablaze,
15 chase them with your fierce storms;
    terrify them with your tempests.
16 Utterly disgrace them
    until they submit to your name, O LORD.
17 Let them be ashamed and terrified forever.
    Make them failures in everything they do,
18 until they learn that you alone are called the
    LORD,
    that you alone are the Most High, supreme
      over all the earth.

## PSALM 84

*For the choir director: A psalm of the descendants of
Korah, to be accompanied by a stringed instrument.\**

1 How lovely is your dwelling place,
    O LORD Almighty.

2 I long, yes, I faint with longing
    to enter the courts of the LORD.
  With my whole being, body and soul,
    I will shout joyfully to
      the living God.
3 Even the sparrow finds a home there,
    and the swallow builds her nest
    and raises her young—
    at a place near your altar,
    O LORD Almighty, my King and my God!
4 How happy are those who can live in your
    house,
    always singing your praises.     *Interlude*

5 Happy are those who are strong in the LORD,
    who set their minds on a pilgrimage to
      Jerusalem.
6 When they walk through the Valley of
    Weeping,\*
    it will become a place of refreshing springs,
    where pools of blessing collect after the rains!
7 They will continue to grow stronger,
    and each of them will appear before God in
      Jerusalem.\*

8 O LORD God Almighty, hear my prayer.
    Listen, O God of Israel.\*     *Interlude*

9 O God, look with favor upon the king, our
    protector!
    Have mercy on the one you have anointed.

10 A single day in your courts
    is better than a thousand anywhere else!
  I would rather be a gatekeeper in the house
    of my God
    than live the good life in the homes of the
      wicked.
11 For the LORD God is our light and protector.
    He gives us grace and glory.

PSALM 85:10-11 The Bible, taken in its entirety,
provides balance for our life. Although both are virtues,
righteousness and peace have different attributes. They
make me think of Jesus, who on the cross satisfied the
justice of God with his sacrifice of love for us. The inter-
section of lines in this art creates a pattern that pictures
the felicity of such harmony.

84:TITLE Hebrew *according to the gittith.*   **84:6** Hebrew *valley of Baca.*   **84:7** Hebrew *Zion.*   **84:8** Hebrew *of Jacob.*

UNFAILING
LOVE AND TRUTH
HAVE MET TOGETHER
RIGHTEOUSNESS
AND PEACE
HAVE KISSED
TRUTH
SPRINGS UP
FROM THE
EARTH
AND
RIGHTEOUSNESS
SMILES DOWN
FROM HEAVEN

No good thing will the LORD withhold
 from those who do what is right.
¹²O LORD Almighty,
 happy are those who trust in you.

## PSALM 85

*For the choir director: A psalm of the descendants
of Korah.*

¹LORD, you have poured out amazing blessings
  on your land!
 You have restored the fortunes of Israel.*
²You have forgiven the guilt of your people—
 yes, you have covered all their sins.
  *Interlude*

³You have withdrawn your fury.
 You have ended your blazing anger.
⁴Now turn to us again, O God of our salvation.
 Put aside your anger against us.
⁵Will you be angry with us always?
 Will you prolong your wrath to distant
  generations?
⁶Won't you revive us again,
 so your people can rejoice in you?
⁷Show us your unfailing love, O LORD,
 and grant us your salvation.

⁸I listen carefully to what God the LORD is
  saying,
 for he speaks peace to his people, his faithful
  ones.
 But let them not return to their foolish
  ways.
⁹Surely his salvation is near to those who honor
  him;
 our land will be filled with his glory.

¹⁰Unfailing love and truth have met together.
 Righteousness and peace have kissed!
¹¹Truth springs up from the earth,
 and righteousness smiles down from
  heaven.
¹²Yes, the LORD pours down his blessings.
 Our land will yield its bountiful crops.
¹³Righteousness goes as a herald before him,
 preparing the way for his steps.

## PSALM 86

*A prayer of David.*

¹Bend down, O LORD, and
  hear my prayer;
 answer me, for I need your
  help.
²Protect me, for I am devoted
  to you.
 Save me, for I serve you and trust you.
 You are my God.
³Be merciful, O Lord,
 for I am calling on you constantly.
⁴Give me happiness, O Lord,
 for my life depends on you.
⁵O Lord, you are so good, so ready to forgive,
 so full of unfailing love for all who ask
  your aid.
⁶Listen closely to my prayer, O LORD;
 hear my urgent cry.
⁷I will call to you whenever trouble strikes,
 and you will answer me.

⁸Nowhere among the pagan gods is there a god
  like you, O Lord.
 There are no other miracles like yours.
⁹All the nations—and you made each one—
 will come and bow before you, Lord;
 they will praise your great and holy
  name.
¹⁰For you are great and perform great miracles.
 You alone are God.

¹¹Teach me your ways, O LORD,
 that I may live according to your truth!
Grant me purity of heart,
 that I may honor you.
¹²With all my heart I will praise you, O Lord
  my God.
 I will give glory to your name forever,
¹³for your love for me is very great.
 You have rescued me from the depths of
  death*!
¹⁴O God, insolent people rise up against me;
 violent people are trying to kill me.
 And you mean nothing to them.

**85:1** Hebrew *of Jacob.*   **86:13** Hebrew *of Sheol.*

¹⁵ But you, O Lord, are a merciful and gracious
   God,
      slow to get angry,
      full of unfailing love and truth.
¹⁶ Look down and have mercy on me.
      Give strength to your servant;
      yes, save me, for I am your servant.
¹⁷ Send me a sign of your favor.
      Then those who hate me will be put to
         shame,
      for you, O LORD, help and comfort me.

## PSALM 87

*A psalm of the descendants of Korah. A song.*

¹ On the holy mountain stands the city founded
      by the LORD.
²    He loves the city of Jerusalem
      more than any other city in Israel.*
³ O city of God,
      what glorious things are said of you!    *Interlude*

⁴ I will record Egypt* and Babylon among those
      who know me—
      also Philistia and Tyre, and even distant
         Ethiopia.*
      They have all become citizens of Jerusalem!
⁵ And it will be said of Jerusalem,*
      "Everyone has become a citizen here."
      And the Most High will personally bless this
         city.
⁶ When the LORD registers the nations,
      he will say, "This one has become a citizen
         of Jerusalem."    *Interlude*

⁷ At all the festivals, the people will sing,
      "The source of my life is in Jerusalem!"

## PSALM 88

*For the choir director: A psalm of the descendants
of Korah, to be sung to the tune "The Suffering of
Affliction." A psalm of Heman the Ezrahite. A song.*

¹ O LORD, God of my salvation,
      I have cried out to you day and night.
² Now hear my prayer;
      listen to my cry.

³ For my life is full of troubles,
      and death draws near.
⁴ I have been dismissed as one who is dead,
      like a strong man with no strength left.
⁵ They have abandoned me to death,
      and I am as good as dead.
   I am forgotten,
      cut off from your care.
⁶ You have thrust me down to the lowest pit,
      into the darkest depths.
⁷ Your anger lies heavy on me;
      wave after wave engulfs me.    *Interlude*

⁸ You have caused my friends to loathe me;
      you have sent them all away.
   I am in a trap with no way of escape.
⁹    My eyes are blinded by my tears.
   Each day I beg for your help, O LORD;
      I lift my pleading hands to you for
         mercy.
¹⁰ Of what use to the dead are your miracles?
      Do the dead get up and praise you?
         *Interlude*

¹¹ Can those in the grave declare your unfailing
      love?
      In the place of destruction, can they
         proclaim your faithfulness?
¹² Can the darkness speak of your miracles?
      Can anyone in the land of forgetfulness talk
         about your righteousness?

¹³ O LORD, I cry out to you.
      I will keep on pleading day by day.
¹⁴ O LORD, why do you reject me?
      Why do you turn your face away
         from me?
¹⁵ I have been sickly and close to death since
         my youth.
      I stand helpless and desperate before your
         terrors.
¹⁶ Your fierce anger has overwhelmed me.
      Your terrors have cut me off.
¹⁷ They swirl around me like floodwaters all
         day long.
      They have encircled me completely.

87:2 Hebrew *He loves the gates of Zion more than all the dwellings of Jacob.*   87:4a Hebrew *Rahab,* the name of a mythical sea monster that represents chaos in ancient
literature. The name is used here as a poetic name for Egypt.   87:4b Hebrew *Cush.*   87:5 Hebrew *Zion.*

<sup>18</sup>You have taken away my companions and
loved ones;
only darkness remains.

## PSALM 89

*A psalm of Ethan the Ezrahite.*

<sup>1</sup>I will sing of the tender mercies of the LORD
forever!
Young and old will hear of your faithfulness.
<sup>2</sup>Your unfailing love will last forever.
Your faithfulness is as enduring as the heavens.

<sup>3</sup>The LORD said, "I have made a solemn
agreement with David, my chosen servant.
I have sworn this oath to him:
<sup>4</sup>'I will establish your descendants as kings
forever;
they will sit on your throne from now until
eternity.'"     *Interlude*

<sup>5</sup>All heaven will praise your miracles, LORD;
myriads of angels will praise you for your
faithfulness.
<sup>6</sup>For who in all of heaven can compare with the
LORD?
What mightiest angel is anything like the
LORD?
<sup>7</sup>The highest angelic powers stand in awe of
God.
He is far more awesome than those who
surround his throne.
<sup>8</sup>O LORD God Almighty!
Where is there anyone as mighty as you,
LORD?
Faithfulness is your very character.

<sup>9</sup>You are the one who rules the oceans.
When their waves rise in fearful storms, you
subdue them.
<sup>10</sup>You are the one who crushed the great sea
monster.*
You scattered your enemies with your
mighty arm.
<sup>11</sup>The heavens are yours, and the earth is yours;
everything in the world is yours—you
created it all.

<sup>12</sup>You created north and south.
Mount Tabor and Mount Hermon praise
your name.
<sup>13</sup>Powerful is your arm!
Strong is your hand!
Your right hand is lifted high in glorious
strength.
<sup>14</sup>Your throne is founded on two strong
pillars—righteousness and justice.
Unfailing love and truth walk before you
as attendants.
<sup>15</sup>Happy are those who hear the joyful call to
worship,
for they will walk in the light of your
presence, LORD.
<sup>16</sup>They rejoice all day long in your wonderful
reputation.
They exult in your righteousness.
<sup>17</sup>You are their glorious strength.
Our power is based on your favor.
<sup>18</sup>Yes, our protection comes from the LORD,
and he, the Holy One of Israel, has given
us our king.

<sup>19</sup>You once spoke in a vision to your prophet
and said,
"I have given help to a warrior.
I have selected him from the common
people to be king.
<sup>20</sup>I have found my servant David.
I have anointed him with my holy oil.
<sup>21</sup>I will steady him,
and I will make him strong.
<sup>22</sup>His enemies will not get the best of him,
nor will the wicked overpower him.
<sup>23</sup>I will beat down his adversaries before him
and destroy those who hate him.
<sup>24</sup>My faithfulness and unfailing love will be with
him,
and he will rise to power because of me.

PSALM 89:5-8, 14   Besides us, the angels also
praise God. We learn here that angels are powerful,
but they pale in comparison to God. Where the words
*righteousness* and *faithfulness* intersect, the pattern that
results is a metaphor for how these traits of God are
integrated.

**89:10** Hebrew *Rahab,* the name of a mythical sea monster that represents chaos in ancient literature.

Myriads of angels will praise you for your faithfulness
For who in all of heaven can compare with the LORD?
What mightiest angel is anything like the LORD?
The highest angelic powers stand in awe of God
He is far more awesome than those who surround his throne

O LORD GOD
ALMIGHTY
WHERE IS THERE
ANYONE AS MIGHTY
AS YOU, LORD?

FAITHFULNESS

IS YOUR VERY CHARACTER

YOUR THRONE IS FOUNDED ON

RIGHTEOUSNESS

TWO STRONG PILLARS

JUSTICE

AND

<sup>25</sup> I will extend his rule from the Mediterranean
    Sea in the west
    to the Tigris and Euphrates rivers in the east.*
<sup>26</sup> And he will say to me, `You are my Father,
    my God, and the Rock of my salvation.'
<sup>27</sup> I will make him my firstborn son,
    the mightiest king on earth.
<sup>28</sup> I will love him and be kind to him forever;
    my covenant with him will never end.
<sup>29</sup> I will preserve an heir for him;
    his throne will be as endless as the days
    of heaven.
<sup>30</sup> But if his sons forsake my law
    and fail to walk in my ways,
<sup>31</sup> if they do not obey my decrees
    and fail to keep my commands,
<sup>32</sup> then I will punish their sin with the rod,
    and their disobedience with beating.
<sup>33</sup> But I will never stop loving him,
    nor let my promise to him fail.
<sup>34</sup> No, I will not break my covenant;
    I will not take back a single word I said.
<sup>35</sup> I have sworn an oath to David,
    and in my holiness I cannot lie:
<sup>36</sup> His dynasty will go on forever;
    his throne is as secure as the sun,
<sup>37</sup>    as eternal as the moon,
    my faithful witness in the sky!"    *Interlude*

<sup>38</sup> But now you have rejected him.
    Why are you so angry with the one you
    chose as king?
<sup>39</sup> You have renounced your covenant with him,
    for you have thrown his crown in the dust.
<sup>40</sup> You have broken down the walls protecting
    him
    and laid in ruins every fort defending him.
<sup>41</sup> Everyone who comes along has robbed him
    while his neighbors mock.
<sup>42</sup> You have strengthened his enemies against him
    and made them all rejoice.
<sup>43</sup> You have made his sword useless
    and have refused to help him in battle.
<sup>44</sup> You have ended his splendor
    and overturned his throne.

**89:25** Hebrew *I will set his hand on the sea, his right hand on the rivers.*

<sup>45</sup> You have made him old before his time
    and publicly disgraced him.    *Interlude*

<sup>46</sup> O LORD, how long will this go on?
    Will you hide yourself forever?
    How long will your anger burn like fire?
<sup>47</sup> Remember how short my life is,
    how empty and futile this human
    existence!
<sup>48</sup> No one can live forever; all will die.
    No one can escape the power of the grave.
    *Interlude*

<sup>49</sup> Lord, where is your unfailing love?
    You promised it to David with a faithful
    pledge.
<sup>50</sup> Consider, Lord, how your servants are disgraced!
    I carry in my heart the insults of so many
    people.
<sup>51</sup> Your enemies have mocked me, O LORD;
    they mock the one you anointed as king.

<sup>52</sup> Blessed be the LORD forever!
    Amen and amen!

BOOK FOUR (Psalms 90–106)

# PSALM 90

*A prayer of Moses, the man of God.*

<sup>1</sup> Lord, through all the generations
    you have been our home!
<sup>2</sup> Before the mountains were created,
    before you made the earth and the
    world,
    you are God, without beginning or end.

<sup>3</sup> You turn people back to dust, saying,
    "Return to dust!"
<sup>4</sup> For you, a thousand years are as yesterday!
    They are like a few hours!

PSALM 90:1-2, 4, 10-14   The various components of a clock combine in different size relationships to reinforce what we learn in the text: Our sense of time is very different from God's. The challenge comes to us: Are we making the best use of our time? At the funeral of a doctor friend I saw the beauty of a life well lived in the testimonies of many who were touched by his compassion.

LORD

THROUGH ALL THE GENERATIONS

YOU HAVE BEEN OUR HOME

SEVENTY YEARS ARE GIVEN TO US

BEFORE THE MOUNTAINS WERE CREATED

SOME MAY EVEN REACH EIGHTY

BEFORE YOU MADE THE EARTH AND THE WORLD

BUT EVEN THE BEST OF THESE YEARS ARE FILLED WITH PAIN AND TROUBLE

YOU ARE GOD

SOON THEY DISAPPEAR AND WE ARE GONE

WITHOUT BEGINNING OR END

WHO CAN COMPREHEND THE POWER OF YOUR ANGER?

FOR YOU

YOUR WRATH IS AS AWESOME AS THE FEAR YOU DESERVE

A THOUSAND YEARS ARE AS YESTERDAY

TEACH US TO MAKE THE MOST OF OUR TIME

THEY ARE LIKE A FEW HOURS

SO THAT WE MAY GROW IN WISDOM

5 You sweep people away like dreams that
disappear

or like grass that springs up in the morning.

6 In the morning it blooms and flourishes,
but by evening it is dry and withered.

7 We wither beneath your anger;
we are overwhelmed by your fury.

8 You spread out our sins before you—
our secret sins—and you see them all.

9 We live our lives beneath your wrath.
We end our lives with a groan.

10 Seventy years are given to us!
Some may even reach eighty.

But even the best of these years are filled with
pain and trouble;

soon they disappear, and we are gone.

11 Who can comprehend the power of your anger?
Your wrath is as awesome as the fear you
deserve.

12 Teach us to make the most of our time,
so that we may grow in wisdom.

13 O LORD, come back to us!
How long will you delay?
Take pity on your servants!

14 Satisfy us in the morning with your unfailing
love,

so we may sing for joy to the end of our
lives.

15 Give us gladness in proportion to our former
misery!

Replace the evil years with good.

16 Let us see your miracles again;
let our children see your glory at work.

17 And may the Lord our God show us his
approval

and make our efforts successful.
Yes, make our efforts successful!

## PSALM 91

1 Those who live in the shelter of the Most
High

will find rest in the shadow of the Almighty.

2 This I declare of the LORD:
He alone is my refuge, my place of safety;
he is my God, and I am trusting him.

3 For he will rescue you from every trap
and protect you from the fatal plague.

4 He will shield you with his wings.
He will shelter you with his feathers.
His faithful promises are your armor and
protection.

5 Do not be afraid of the terrors of the night,
nor fear the dangers of the day,

6 nor dread the plague that stalks in darkness,
nor the disaster that strikes at midday.

7 Though a thousand fall at your side,
though ten thousand are dying around you,
these evils will not touch you.

8 But you will see it with your eyes;
you will see how the wicked are punished.

9 If you make the LORD your refuge,
if you make the Most High your shelter,

10 no evil will conquer you;
no plague will come near your dwelling.

11 For he orders his angels
to protect you wherever you go.

12 They will hold you with their hands
to keep you from striking your foot on a
stone.

13 You will trample down lions and poisonous
snakes;

you will crush fierce lions and serpents under
your feet!

14 The LORD says, "I will rescue those who love
me.

I will protect those who trust in my name.

15 When they call on me, I will answer;
I will be with them in trouble.
I will rescue them and honor them.

16 I will satisfy them with a long life
and give them my salvation."

## PSALM 92

*A psalm to be sung on the LORD's Day. A song.*

1 It is good to give thanks to the LORD,
to sing praises to the Most High.

2 It is good to proclaim your unfailing love
in the morning,

your faithfulness in the evening,

³accompanied by the harp and lute
  and the harmony of the lyre.
⁴You thrill me, LORD, with all you have done
    for me!
  I sing for joy because of what you have done.

⁵O LORD, what great miracles you do!
  And how deep are your thoughts.
⁶Only an ignorant person would not know this!
  Only a fool would not understand it.
⁷Although the wicked flourish like weeds,
  and evildoers blossom with success,
    there is only eternal destruction ahead
    of them.
⁸But you are exalted in the heavens.
  You, O LORD, continue forever.
⁹Your enemies, LORD, will surely perish;
  all evildoers will be scattered.

¹⁰But you have made me as strong as a wild
    bull.
  How refreshed I am by your power!
¹¹With my own eyes I have seen the downfall
    of my enemies;
  with my own ears I have heard the defeat
    of my wicked opponents.
¹²But the godly will flourish like palm trees
  and grow strong like the cedars of Lebanon.
¹³For they are transplanted into the LORD's own
    house.
  They flourish in the courts of our God.
¹⁴Even in old age they will still produce fruit;
  they will remain vital and green.
¹⁵They will declare, "The LORD is just!
  He is my rock!
  There is nothing but goodness in him!"

## PSALM 93

¹The LORD is king! He is robed in majesty.
  Indeed, the LORD is robed in majesty and
    armed with strength.
The world is firmly established;
  it cannot be shaken.

²Your throne, O LORD, has been established
    from time immemorial.
  You yourself are from the everlasting past.

PSALM 90:16-17   I identify with this prayer for
God to show his power—for the strengthening of our
own faith and for the sake of our children. The fish
came to mind from Jesus' miracle of feeding the five
thousand. I pray also that the ranks of his followers
may increase.

³The mighty oceans have roared, O LORD.
  The mighty oceans roar like thunder;
    the mighty oceans roar as they pound
    the shore.
⁴But mightier than the violent raging of the
    seas,
  mightier than the breakers on the shore—
    the LORD above is mightier than these!
⁵Your royal decrees cannot be changed.
  The nature of your reign, O LORD, is
    holiness forever.

## PSALM 94

¹O LORD, the God to whom vengeance
belongs,
O God of vengeance, let your glorious
justice be seen!
²Arise, O judge of the earth.
Sentence the proud to the penalties they
deserve.
³How long, O LORD?
How long will the wicked be allowed to
gloat?
⁴Hear their arrogance!
How these evildoers boast!
⁵They oppress your people, LORD,
hurting those you love.
⁶They kill widows and foreigners
and murder orphans.
⁷"The LORD isn't looking," they say,
"and besides, the God of Israel* doesn't
care."

⁸Think again, you fools!
When will you finally catch on?
⁹Is the one who made your ears deaf?
Is the one who formed your eyes blind?
¹⁰He punishes the nations—won't he also
punish you?
He knows everything—doesn't he also know
what you are doing?
¹¹The LORD knows people's thoughts,
that they are worthless!

¹²Happy are those whom you discipline,
LORD,
and those whom you teach from your law.
¹³You give them relief from troubled times
until a pit is dug for the wicked.
¹⁴The LORD will not reject his people;
he will not abandon his own special
possession.
¹⁵Judgment will come again for the righteous,
and those who are upright will have a
reward.

¹⁶Who will protect me from the wicked?
Who will stand up for me against evildoers?

¹⁷Unless the LORD had helped me,
I would soon have died.
¹⁸I cried out, "I'm slipping!"
and your unfailing love, O LORD,
supported me.
¹⁹When doubts filled my mind,
your comfort gave me renewed hope and
cheer.

²⁰Can unjust leaders claim that God is on their
side—
leaders who permit injustice by their laws?
²¹They attack the righteous
and condemn the innocent to death.
²²But the LORD is my fortress;
my God is a mighty rock where I can hide.
²³God will make the sins of evil people fall
back upon them.
He will destroy them for their sins.
The LORD our God will destroy them.

## PSALM 95

¹Come, let us sing to the LORD!
Let us give a joyous shout to the rock of our
salvation!
²Let us come before him with thanksgiving.
Let us sing him psalms of praise.
³For the LORD is a great God,
the great King above all gods.
⁴He owns the depths of the earth,
and even the mightiest mountains are his.
⁵The sea belongs to him, for he made it.
His hands formed the dry land, too.

⁶Come, let us worship and bow down.
Let us kneel before the LORD our maker,
⁷ for he is our God.
We are the people he watches over,
the sheep under his care.

Oh, that you would listen to his voice today!

PSALM 91:1-4  To be in God's protection is a
good place to be. This is the truth: There is no security
anywhere else. So I've chosen to place my life in his
hands. Here I worked with the beautiful imagery of a
bird's wing, which is strong enough to carry and whose
feathers are gentle enough for shelter.

**94:7** Hebrew *of Jacob.*

Those
who live
in the
shelter of the
Most High
will find rest in the
shadow of the Almighty.
This I declare of the LORD:
He alone is my refuge,
my place of safety;
he is my God, and I am trusting him.
For he will rescue you from every trap
and protect you from the fatal plague.
He will shield you with his wings.
He will shelter you with his feathers.

HIS FAITHFUL PROMISES ARE
YOUR ARMOR AND PROTECTION

8 The LORD says, "Don't harden your hearts as
Israel did at Meribah,
as they did at Massah in the wilderness.
9 For there your ancestors tried my patience;
they courted my wrath though they had
seen my many miracles.
10 For forty years I was angry with them, and
I said,
`They are a people whose hearts turn away
from me.
They refuse to do what I tell them.'
11 So in my anger I made a vow:
'They will never enter my place of rest.'"

## PSALM 96

1 Sing a new song to the LORD!
Let the whole earth sing to the LORD!
2 Sing to the LORD; bless his name.
Each day proclaim the good news that he saves.
3 Publish his glorious deeds among the
nations.
Tell everyone about the amazing things
he does.
4 Great is the LORD! He is most worthy of
praise!
He is to be revered above all the gods.
5 The gods of other nations are merely idols,
but the LORD made the heavens!
6 Honor and majesty surround him;
strength and beauty are in his sanctuary.

7 O nations of the world, recognize the LORD;
recognize that the LORD is glorious and
strong.
8 Give to the LORD the glory he deserves!
Bring your offering and come to worship
him.
9 Worship the LORD in all his holy splendor.
Let all the earth tremble before him.
10 Tell all the nations that the LORD is king.
The world is firmly established and cannot
be shaken.
He will judge all peoples fairly.

11 Let the heavens be glad, and let the earth
rejoice!

97:8 Hebrew *Zion.*

Let the sea and everything in it shout his
praise!
12 Let the fields and their crops burst forth
with joy!
Let the trees of the forest rustle with
praise
13 before the LORD!
For the LORD is coming!
He is coming to judge the earth.
He will judge the world with righteousness
and all the nations with his truth.

## PSALM 97

1 The LORD is king! Let the earth rejoice!
Let the farthest islands be glad.
2 Clouds and darkness surround him.
Righteousness and justice are the
foundation of his throne.
3 Fire goes forth before him
and burns up all his foes.
4 His lightning flashes out across the world.
The earth sees and trembles.
5 The mountains melt like wax before the
LORD,
before the Lord of all the earth.
6 The heavens declare his righteousness;
every nation sees his glory.
7 Those who worship idols are disgraced—
all who brag about their worthless
gods—
for every god must bow to him.
8 Jerusalem* has heard and rejoiced,
and all the cities of Judah are glad
because of your justice, LORD!
9 For you, O LORD, are most high over all the
earth;
you are exalted far above all gods.

PSALM 92:12-14   Recently I transplanted a volunteer tree in our yard because it needed a new location. The trunk was only two inches in diameter, but I had to dig down two feet before I could dislodge the taproot. Despite the trauma to the tree, I know that in the coming years it will flourish in better conditions. Those who love the Lord and are transplanted into his own house will likewise be fruitful and gain strength.

The godly will flourish like palm trees and grow strong like the cedars of Lebanon

For they are transplanted into the LORD's own house

They flourish in the courts of our God

Even They in old age they will still produce fruit

will remain vital and green

¹⁰You who love the LORD, hate evil!
   He protects the lives of his godly people
   and rescues them from the power of the
      wicked.
¹¹Light shines on the godly,
   and joy on those who do right.
¹²May all who are godly be happy in the LORD
   and praise his holy name!

## PSALM 98

*A psalm.*

¹Sing a new song to the LORD,
   for he has done wonderful deeds.
 He has won a mighty victory
   by his power and holiness.
²The LORD has announced his victory
   and has revealed his righteousness to every
      nation!
³He has remembered his promise to love and
   be faithful to Israel.
 The whole earth has seen the salvation
   of our God.

⁴Shout to the LORD, all the earth;
   break out in praise and sing for joy!
⁵Sing your praise to the LORD with the harp,
   with the harp and melodious song,
⁶   with trumpets and the sound of the ram's
      horn.
 Make a joyful symphony before the LORD,
   the King!

⁷Let the sea and everything in it shout his
   praise!
 Let the earth and all living things join in.
⁸   Let the rivers clap their hands in glee!
 Let the hills sing out their songs of joy
⁹      before the LORD.
 For the LORD is coming to judge the earth.
   He will judge the world with justice,
   and the nations with fairness.

## PSALM 99

¹The LORD is king!
   Let the nations tremble!

99:2 Hebrew *Zion.*  99:4 Hebrew *Jacob.*

He sits on his throne between the cherubim.
   Let the whole earth quake!
²The LORD sits in majesty in Jerusalem,*
   supreme above all the nations.
³Let them praise your great and awesome name.
   Your name is holy!
⁴Mighty king, lover of justice,
   you have established fairness.
 You have acted with justice
   and righteousness throughout Israel.*
⁵Exalt the LORD our God!
   Bow low before his feet, for he is holy!

⁶Moses and Aaron were among his priests;
   Samuel also called on his name.
 They cried to the LORD for help,
   and he answered them.
⁷He spoke to them from the pillar of cloud,
   and they followed the decrees and principles
      he gave them.
⁸O LORD our God, you answered them.
   You were a forgiving God,
   but you punished them when they went
      wrong.

⁹Exalt the LORD our God
   and worship at his holy mountain in
      Jerusalem,
   for the LORD our God is holy!

## PSALM 100

*A psalm of thanksgiving.*

¹Shout with joy to the LORD, O earth!
²   Worship the LORD with gladness.
   Come before him, singing with joy.
³Acknowledge that the LORD is God!
   He made us, and we are his.
   We are his people, the sheep of his
      pasture.

🖋  PSALM 96:4-5, 7-8, 13   As an artist, I can use
my creative energies to bring honor to God. Banners,
stained glass, and illuminated manuscripts are part of
this same tradition. The way we present ourselves, our
homes, and our workplaces can also be a statement of
whom we represent. When the Lord returns to earth,
will he find us in the practice of praise?

# GREAT

IS THE LORD
HE IS MOST
WORTHY OF PRAISE
HE IS TO BE REVERED
ABOVE ALL THE GODS.
THE GODS OF
OTHER NATIONS
ARE MERELY IDOLS
BUT THE LORD
MADE THE HEAVENS
O NATIONS
OF THE WORLD
RECOGNIZE THE LORD
GIVE TO THE LORD
THE GLORY HE DESERVES

FOR THE LORD IS COMING
HE IS COMING TO
JUDGE THE EARTH
HE WILL JUDGE THE WORLD
WITH RIGHTEOUSNESS
AND ALL THE NATIONS
WITH HIS TRUTH

4 Enter his gates with thanksgiving;
  go into his courts with praise.
  Give thanks to him and bless his name.
5 For the LORD is good.
  His unfailing love continues forever,
  and his faithfulness continues to each
    generation.

## PSALM 101

*A psalm of David.*

1 I will sing of your love and justice.
  I will praise you, LORD, with songs.
2 I will be careful to live a blameless life—
  when will you come to my aid?
  I will lead a life of integrity
  in my own home.
3 I will refuse to look at
  anything vile and vulgar.
  I hate all crooked dealings;
  I will have nothing to do with them.
4 I will reject perverse ideas
  and stay away from every evil.
5 I will not tolerate people who slander their
    neighbors.
  I will not endure conceit and pride.

6 I will keep a protective eye on the godly,
  so they may dwell with me in safety.
  Only those who are above reproach
  will be allowed to serve me.
7 I will not allow deceivers to serve me,
  and liars will not be allowed to enter my
    presence.
8 My daily task will be to ferret out criminals
  and free the city of the LORD from their
    grip.

## PSALM 102

*A prayer of one overwhelmed with trouble, pouring out problems before the LORD.*

1 LORD, hear my prayer!
  Listen to my plea!
2 Don't turn away from me
  in my time of distress.

**102:13** Hebrew *Zion;* also in 102:16.

Bend down your ear
  and answer me quickly when I call to you,
3  for my days disappear like smoke,
  and my bones burn like red-hot coals.
4 My heart is sick, withered like grass,
  and I have lost my appetite.
5 Because of my groaning,
  I am reduced to skin and bones.
6 I am like an owl in the desert,
  like a lonely owl in a far-off wilderness.
7 I lie awake,
  lonely as a solitary bird on the roof.
8 My enemies taunt me day after day.
  They mock and curse me.
9 I eat ashes instead of my food.
  My tears run down into my drink
10 because of your anger and wrath.
  For you have picked me up and thrown
    me out.
11 My life passes as swiftly as the evening shadows.
  I am withering like grass.

12 But you, O LORD, will rule forever.
  Your fame will endure to every generation.
13 You will arise and have mercy on Jerusalem*—
  and now is the time to pity her,
  now is the time you promised to help.
14 For your people love every stone in her walls
  and show favor even to the dust in her streets.
15 And the nations will tremble before the LORD.
  The kings of the earth will tremble before
    his glory.
16 For the LORD will rebuild Jerusalem.
  He will appear in his glory.
17 He will listen to the prayers of the destitute.
  He will not reject their pleas.

18 Let this be recorded for future generations,
  so that a nation yet to be created will praise
    the LORD.

PSALM 100  The focus of this psalm is on entering God's presence, acknowledging his rightful position, depending on him, and being grateful to him. The source of the background is from a synagogue in the Middle East. The layout of this piece is symmetrical and classically arched to invite you to come in!

Shout with joy
to the LORD, O earth
Worship the LORD with gladness
Come before him, singing with joy
ACKNOWLEDGE THAT
THE LORD IS GOD

he made us, and we are his
We are his people, the sheep of his pasture
Enter his gates with thanksgiving
go into his courts with praise
Give thanks to him and bless his name
FOR THE LORD IS GOOD
his unfailing love continues forever
and his faithfulness continues to each generation

¹⁹Tell them the LORD looked down
   from his heavenly sanctuary.
   He looked to the earth from heaven
²⁰   to hear the groans of the prisoners,
   to release those condemned to die.
²¹And so the LORD's fame will be celebrated
   in Zion,
   his praises in Jerusalem,
²²when multitudes gather together
   and kingdoms come to worship the LORD.

²³He has cut me down in midlife,
   shortening my days.
²⁴But I cried to him, "My God, who lives
   forever,
   don't take my life while I am still so young!
²⁵In ages past you laid the foundation of the
   earth,
   and the heavens are the work of your hands.
²⁶Even they will perish, but you remain
   forever;
   they will wear out like old clothing.
   You will change them like a garment,
   and they will fade away.
²⁷But you are always the same;
   your years never end.
²⁸The children of your people
   will live in security.
   Their children's children
   will thrive in your presence."

## PSALM 103

*A psalm of David.*

¹Praise the LORD, I tell myself;
   with my whole heart, I will praise his holy
   name.
²Praise the LORD, I tell myself,
   and never forget the good things he does
   for me.
³He forgives all my sins
   and heals all my diseases.
⁴He ransoms me from death
   and surrounds me with love and tender
   mercies.
⁵He fills my life with good things.
   My youth is renewed like the eagle's!

⁶The LORD gives righteousness
   and justice to all who are treated unfairly.
⁷He revealed his character to Moses
   and his deeds to the people of Israel.
⁸The LORD is merciful and gracious;
   he is slow to get angry and full of unfailing
   love.
⁹He will not constantly accuse us,
   nor remain angry forever.
¹⁰He has not punished us for all our sins,
   nor does he deal with us as we deserve.
¹¹For his unfailing love toward those who fear
   him
   is as great as the height of the heavens above
   the earth.
¹²He has removed our rebellious acts
   as far away from us as the east is from the
   west.
¹³The LORD is like a father to his children,
   tender and compassionate to those who fear
   him.
¹⁴For he understands how weak we are;
   he knows we are only dust.
¹⁵Our days on earth are like grass;
   like wildflowers, we bloom and die.
¹⁶The wind blows, and we are gone—
   as though we had never been here.
¹⁷But the love of the LORD remains forever
   with those who fear him.
   His salvation extends to the children's children
¹⁸   of those who are faithful to his covenant,
   of those who obey his commandments!

¹⁹The LORD has made the heavens his
   throne;
   from there he rules over everything.
²⁰Praise the LORD, you angels of his,
   you mighty creatures who carry out his
   plans,
   listening for each of his commands.
²¹Yes, praise the LORD, you armies of angels
   who serve him and do his will!
²²Praise the LORD, everything he has created,
   everywhere in his kingdom.
   As for me—I, too, will praise the LORD.

## PSALM 104

¹Praise the LORD, I tell myself;
　O LORD my God, how great you are!
　You are robed with honor and with majesty;
² 　you are dressed in a robe of light.
　You stretch out the starry curtain of the
　　　heavens;
³ 　you lay out the rafters of your home in the
　　　rain clouds.
　You make the clouds your chariots;
　　you ride upon the wings of the wind.
⁴The winds are your messengers;
　　flames of fire are your servants.

⁵You placed the world on its foundation
　　so it would never be moved.
⁶You clothed the earth with floods of water,
　　water that covered even the mountains.
⁷At the sound of your rebuke, the water fled;
　　at the sound of your thunder, it fled away.
⁸Mountains rose and valleys sank
　　to the levels you decreed.
⁹Then you set a firm boundary for the seas,
　　so they would never again cover the earth.

¹⁰You make the springs pour water into
　　　ravines,
　　so streams gush down from the mountains.
¹¹They provide water for all the animals,
　　and the wild donkeys quench their thirst.
¹²The birds nest beside the streams
　　and sing among the branches of the trees.
¹³You send rain on the mountains from your
　　　heavenly home,
　　and you fill the earth with the fruit of your
　　　labor.
¹⁴You cause grass to grow for the cattle.
　　You cause plants to grow for people to use.
　　You allow them to produce food from the
　　　earth—
¹⁵ 　wine to make them glad,
　　olive oil as lotion for their skin,
　　and bread to give them strength.
¹⁶The trees of the LORD are well cared for—
　　the cedars of Lebanon that he planted.
¹⁷There the birds make their nests,
　　and the storks make their homes in the firs.

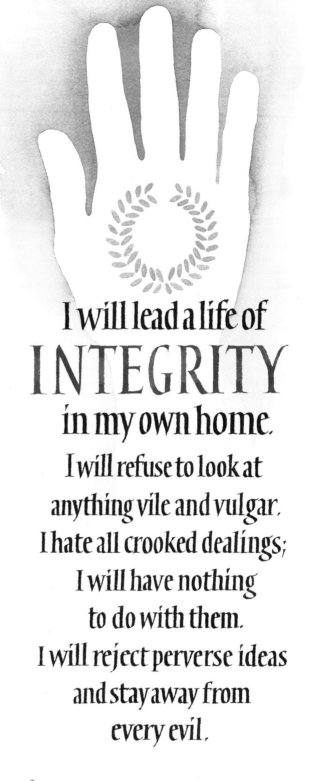

I will lead a life of
# INTEGRITY
in my own home.
I will refuse to look at
anything vile and vulgar.
I hate all crooked dealings;
I will have nothing
to do with them.
I will reject perverse ideas
and stay away from
every evil.

PSALM 101:2-4   The Psalms are full of promises
that we love to read. But this text reminds us that we
also have a responsibility to choose the right path. I
made the association here of taking an oath, in this
case, before the highest court.

18 High in the mountains are pastures for the
  wild goats,
    and the rocks form a refuge for rock badgers.*
19 You made the moon to mark the seasons
    and the sun that knows when to set.
20 You send the darkness, and it becomes night,
    when all the forest animals prowl about.
21 Then the young lions roar for their food,
    but they are dependent on God.
22 At dawn they slink back
    into their dens to rest.
23 Then people go off to their work;
    they labor until the evening shadows fall
      again.

24 O LORD, what a variety of things you have
  made!
    In wisdom you have made them all.
    The earth is full of your creatures.
25 Here is the ocean, vast and wide,
    teeming with life of every kind,
      both great and small.
26 See the ships sailing along,
    and Leviathan, which you made to play
      in the sea.
27 Every one of these depends on you
    to give them their food as they need it.
28 When you supply it, they gather it.
    You open your hand to feed them, and they
      are satisfied.
29 But if you turn away from them, they panic.
    When you take away their breath, they die
      and turn again to dust.
30 When you send your Spirit, new life is born
    to replenish all the living of the earth.

31 May the glory of the LORD last forever!
    The LORD rejoices in all he has made!
32 The earth trembles at his glance;
    the mountains burst into flame at his
      touch.
33 I will sing to the LORD as long as I live.
    I will praise my God to my last breath!
34 May he be pleased by all these thoughts
    about him,
    for I rejoice in the LORD.

35 Let all sinners vanish from the face of the earth;
    let the wicked disappear forever.
  As for me—I will praise the LORD!

Praise the LORD!

## PSALM 105

1 Give thanks to the LORD and proclaim his
  greatness.
    Let the whole world know what he has done.
2 Sing to him; yes, sing his praises.
    Tell everyone about his miracles.
3 Exult in his holy name;
    O worshipers of the LORD, rejoice!
4 Search for the LORD and for his strength,
    and keep on searching.
5 Think of the wonderful works he has done,
    the miracles and the judgments he handed
      down,
6 O children of Abraham, God's servant,
    O descendants of Jacob, God's chosen one.
7 He is the LORD our God.
    His rule is seen throughout the land.
8 He always stands by his covenant—
    the commitment he made to a thousand
      generations.
9 This is the covenant he made with Abraham
    and the oath he swore to Isaac.
10 He confirmed it to Jacob as a decree,
    to the people of Israel as a never-ending
      treaty:
11 "I will give you the land of Canaan
    as your special possession."

12 He said this when they were few in number,
    a tiny group of strangers in Canaan.
13 They wandered back and forth between
      nations,
    from one kingdom to another.

PSALM 103:8-18   In this piece, I was thinking
about the rings of an old tree. One day of faithfulness
may not seem very significant, but what an image of
strength when the fear of God is held throughout an
entire lifetime and transferred to another generation.
This is an example of using one style of lettering—
italic—and applying variations to its use for the visual
interpretation of the text.

**104:18** Or *coneys,* or *hyraxes.*

The LORD is merciful and gracious,
He is slow to get angry and full of unfailing love
He will not constantly accuse us, nor remain angry forever
He has not punished us for all our sins
nor does he deal with us as we deserve
For his unfailing love toward those who fear him
is AS GREAT AS THE HEIGHT OF THE HEAVENS above the earth
He has removed our rebellious acts
as far away from us
as the east is from the west

The LORD is like a father to his children,
tender and compassionate to those who fear him.
For he understands how weak we are.
He knows we are only dust.
Our days on earth are like grass;
like wildflowers, we bloom and die.
The wind blows, and we are gone,
as though we had never been here.

BUT the love of the LORD remains forever
with those who fear him.
His salvation extends to the children's children
of those who are faithful to his covenant
of those who obey his commandments!

14 Yet he did not let anyone oppress them.
  He warned kings on their behalf:
15 "Do not touch these people I have chosen,
  and do not hurt my prophets."
16 He called for a famine on the land of Canaan,
  cutting off its food supply.
17 Then he sent someone to Egypt ahead of
    them—
  Joseph, who was sold as a slave.
18 There in prison, they bruised his feet with
    fetters
  and placed his neck in an iron collar.
19 Until the time came to fulfill his word,
  the LORD tested Joseph's character.
20 Then Pharaoh sent for him and set him free;
  the ruler of the nation opened his prison
    door.
21 Joseph was put in charge of all the king's
    household;
  he became ruler over all the king's
    possessions.
22 He could instruct the king's aides as he pleased
  and teach the king's advisers.

23 Then Israel arrived in Egypt;
  Jacob lived as a foreigner in the land of
    Ham.
24 And the LORD multiplied the people of Israel
  until they became too mighty for their
    enemies.
25 Then he turned the Egyptians against the
    Israelites,
  and they plotted against the LORD's servants.

26 But the LORD sent Moses his servant,
  along with Aaron, whom he had chosen.
27 They performed miraculous signs among the
    Egyptians,
  and miracles in the land of Ham.
28 The LORD blanketed Egypt in darkness,
  for they had defied his commands to let
    his people go.
29 He turned the nation's water into blood,
  poisoning all the fish.
30 Then frogs overran the land;
  they were found even in the king's private
    rooms.

31 When he spoke, flies descended on the Egyptians,
  and gnats swarmed across Egypt.
32 Instead of rain, he sent murderous hail,
  and flashes of lightning overwhelmed the land.
33 He ruined their grapevines and fig trees
  and shattered all the trees.
34 He spoke, and hordes of locusts came—
  locusts beyond number.
35 They ate up everything green in the land,
  destroying all the crops.
36 Then he killed the oldest child in each
    Egyptian home,
  the pride and joy of each family.

37 But he brought his people safely out of Egypt,
  loaded with silver and gold;
  there were no sick or feeble people among
    them.
38 Egypt was glad when they were gone,
  for the dread of them was great.
39 The LORD spread out a cloud above them as a
    covering
  and gave them a great fire to light the
    darkness.
40 They asked for meat, and he sent them quail;
  he gave them manna—bread from heaven.
41 He opened up a rock, and water gushed out
  to form a river through the dry and barren
    land.
42 For he remembered his sacred promise
  to Abraham his servant.
43 So he brought his people out of Egypt with joy,
  his chosen ones with rejoicing.
44 He gave his people the lands of pagan nations,
  and they harvested crops that others had
    planted.
45 All this happened so they would follow his
    principles
  and obey his laws.

Praise the LORD!

PSALM 104:24, 31   The variety of patterns, colors, shapes, and personalities in creation reveals God's extravagance, playfulness, mystery, and limitless imagination. These verses remind me that God is the author of diversity and that we miss out if we close our mind to what is different from ourselves.

O LORD
what a
variety
of things
YOU
have **MADE**
In WISDOM
YOU have
**MADE** all
them all all
all
THE
earth
is *full* of
YOUR
CREATURES

The LORD rejoices in all he has made

# PSALM 106

¹Praise the LORD!

Give thanks to the LORD, for he is good!
    His faithful love endures forever.
²Who can list the glorious miracles of the
    LORD?
    Who can ever praise him half enough?
³Happy are those who deal justly with others
    and always do what is right.

⁴Remember me, too, LORD, when you show
    favor to your people;
    come to me with your salvation.
⁵Let me share in the prosperity of your chosen
    ones.
    Let me rejoice in the joy of your people;
    let me praise you with those who are your
    heritage.

⁶Both we and our ancestors have sinned.
    We have done wrong! We have acted
    wickedly!
⁷Our ancestors in Egypt
    were not impressed by the LORD's miracles.
    They soon forgot his many acts of kindness
    to them.
    Instead, they rebelled against him at the
    Red Sea.*
⁸Even so, he saved them—
    to defend the honor of his name
    and to demonstrate his mighty power.
⁹He commanded the Red Sea* to divide, and
    a dry path appeared.
    He led Israel across the sea bottom that was
    as dry as a desert.
¹⁰So he rescued them from their enemies
    and redeemed them from their foes.
¹¹Then the water returned and covered their
    enemies;
    not one of them survived.
¹²Then at last his people believed his promises.
    Then they finally sang his praise.

¹³Yet how quickly they forgot what he had
    done!
    They wouldn't wait for his counsel!

¹⁴In the wilderness, their desires ran wild,
    testing God's patience in that dry land.
¹⁵So he gave them what they asked for,
    but he sent a plague along with it.
¹⁶The people in the camp were jealous of Moses
    and envious of Aaron, the LORD's holy priest.
¹⁷Because of this, the earth opened up;
    it swallowed Dathan
    and buried Abiram and the other rebels.
¹⁸Fire fell upon their followers;
    a flame consumed the wicked.

¹⁹The people made a calf at Mount Sinai*;
    they bowed before an image made of gold.
²⁰They traded their glorious God
    for a statue of a grass-eating ox!
²¹They forgot God, their savior,
    who had done such great things in Egypt—
²²such wonderful things in that land,
    such awesome deeds at the Red Sea.
²³So he declared he would destroy them.
    But Moses, his chosen one, stepped between
    the LORD and the people.
    He begged him to turn from his anger and
    not destroy them.

²⁴The people refused to enter the pleasant land,
    for they wouldn't believe his promise to care
    for them.
²⁵Instead, they grumbled in their tents
    and refused to obey the LORD.
²⁶Therefore, he swore
    that he would kill them in the wilderness,
²⁷that he would scatter their descendants among
    the nations,
    exiling them to distant lands.

²⁸Then our ancestors joined in the worship
    of Baal at Peor;
    they even ate sacrifices offered to the dead!
²⁹They angered the LORD with all these things,
    so a plague broke out among them.
³⁰But Phinehas had the courage to step in,
    and the plague was stopped.
³¹So he has been regarded as a righteous man
    ever since that time.

106:7 Hebrew *at the sea, the sea of reeds.* 106:9 Hebrew *sea of reeds;* also in 106:22. 106:19 Hebrew *at Horeb,* another name for Sinai.

32 At Meribah, too, they angered the LORD,
   causing Moses serious trouble.
33 They made Moses angry,*
   and he spoke foolishly.

34 Israel failed to destroy the nations in the land,
   as the LORD had told them to.
35 Instead, they mingled among the pagans
   and adopted their evil customs.
36 They worshiped their idols,
   and this led to their downfall.
37 They even sacrificed their sons
   and their daughters to the demons.
38 They shed innocent blood,
   the blood of their sons and daughters.
 By sacrificing them to the idols of Canaan,
   they polluted the land with murder.
39 They defiled themselves by their evil deeds,
   and their love of idols was adultery in the
      LORD's sight.

40 That is why the LORD's anger burned against
      his people,
   and he abhorred his own special possession.
41 He handed them over to pagan nations,
   and those who hated them ruled over them.
42 Their enemies crushed them
   and brought them under their cruel power.
43 Again and again he delivered them,
   but they continued to rebel against him,
   and they were finally destroyed by their sin.
44 Even so, he pitied them in their distress
   and listened to their cries.
45 He remembered his covenant with them
   and relented because of his unfailing love.
46 He even caused their captors
   to treat them with kindness.

47 O LORD our God, save us!
   Gather us back from among the nations,
 so we can thank your holy name
   and rejoice and praise you.
48 Blessed be the LORD, the God of Israel,
   from everlasting to everlasting!
 Let all the people say, "Amen!"

 Praise the LORD!

106:33 Hebrew *They embittered his spirit.*

THEY TRADED *their glorious* GOD FOR a statue of a grass-eating ox

PSALM 106:20   This is a disturbingly familiar description of our preoccupation with things of our own making. We forget the one who is the source of all things including our creative powers. I like to use gold leaf as illustrated here in reference to the divine. This is because it does not tarnish, which is evident in medieval manuscripts.

BOOK FIVE (Psalms 107–150)
## PSALM 107
1 Give thanks to the LORD, for he is good!
   His faithful love endures forever.
2 Has the LORD redeemed you? Then speak out!
   Tell others he has saved you from your
      enemies.

³For he has gathered the exiles from many lands,
 from east and west, from north and south.

⁴Some wandered in the desert,
 lost and homeless.
⁵Hungry and thirsty,
 they nearly died.
⁶"LORD, help!" they cried in their trouble,
 and he rescued them from their distress.
⁷He led them straight to safety,
 to a city where they could live.
⁸Let them praise the LORD for his great love
 and for all his wonderful deeds to them.
⁹For he satisfies the thirsty
 and fills the hungry with good things.

¹⁰Some sat in darkness and deepest gloom,
 miserable prisoners in chains.
¹¹They rebelled against the words of God,
 scorning the counsel of the Most High.
¹²That is why he broke them with hard labor;
 they fell, and no one helped them rise again.
¹³"LORD, help!" they cried in their trouble,
 and he saved them from their distress.
¹⁴He led them from the darkness and deepest
 gloom;
 he snapped their chains.
¹⁵Let them praise the LORD for his great love
 and for all his wonderful deeds to them.
¹⁶For he broke down their prison gates of
 bronze;
 he cut apart their bars of iron.

¹⁷Some were fools in their rebellion;
 they suffered for their sins.
¹⁸Their appetites were gone,
 and death was near.
¹⁹"LORD, help!" they cried in their trouble,
 and he saved them from their distress.
²⁰He spoke, and they were healed—
 snatched from the door of death.
²¹Let them praise the LORD for his great love
 and for all his wonderful deeds to them.
²²Let them offer sacrifices of thanksgiving
 and sing joyfully about his glorious acts.

²³Some went off in ships,
 plying the trade routes of the world.

²⁴They, too, observed the LORD's power in
 action,
 his impressive works on the deepest seas.
²⁵He spoke, and the winds rose,
 stirring up the waves.
²⁶Their ships were tossed to the heavens
 and sank again to the depths;
 the sailors cringed in terror.
²⁷They reeled and staggered like drunkards
 and were at their wits' end.
²⁸"LORD, help!" they cried in their trouble,
 and he saved them from their distress.
²⁹He calmed the storm to a whisper
 and stilled the waves.
³⁰What a blessing was that stillness
 as he brought them safely into harbor!
³¹Let them praise the LORD for his great love
 and for all his wonderful deeds to them.
³²Let them exalt him publicly before the
 congregation
 and before the leaders of the nation.

³³He changes rivers into deserts,
 and springs of water into dry land.
³⁴He turns the fruitful land into salty wastelands,
 because of the wickedness of those who live
 there.
³⁵But he also turns deserts into pools of water,
 the dry land into flowing springs.
³⁶He brings the hungry to settle there
 and build their cities.
³⁷They sow their fields, plant their vineyards,
 and harvest their bumper crops.
³⁸How he blesses them!
 They raise large families there,
 and their herds of cattle increase.

³⁹When they decrease in number and become
 impoverished
 through oppression, trouble, and sorrow,

PSALM 107:1-2, 9, 43   The universal craving for
satisfaction can be met by the Lord. Those of us who
have experienced this for ourselves have a responsibility
to let others know, so I created a megaphone-like
design for this text. The last verse speaks of God's deliverance of his chosen people throughout their history. In
our own day we can see this in the remarkable reset-
tling of Israel in 1948.

Give thanks to the LORD, for he is good!

His faithful love endures forever

Has the LORD redeemed you?
THEN SPEAK OUT

Tell others he has saved you
others others
others others
others
from your enemies

For he satisfies the thirsty
and fills the hungry with good things

Those who are wise will take all this to heart

They will see in our history
the faithful love of the LORD

40 the LORD pours contempt on their princes,
 causing them to wander in trackless
 wastelands.
41 But he rescues the poor from their distress
 and increases their families like vast flocks of
 sheep.
42 The godly will see these things and be glad,
 while the wicked are stricken silent.
43 Those who are wise will take all this to heart;
 they will see in our history the faithful love
 of the LORD.

## PSALM 108

*A psalm of David. A song.*

1 My heart is confident in you, O God;
 no wonder I can sing your praises!
 Wake up, my soul!
2  Wake up, O harp and lyre!
 I will waken the dawn with my song.
3 I will thank you, LORD, in front of all the
 people.
 I will sing your praises among the nations.
4 For your unfailing love is higher than the
 heavens.
 Your faithfulness reaches to the clouds.
5 Be exalted, O God, above the highest heavens.
 May your glory shine over all the earth.

6 Use your strong right arm to save me,
 and rescue your beloved people.
7 God has promised this by his holiness*:
 "I will divide up Shechem with joy.
 I will measure out the valley of Succoth.
8 Gilead is mine,
 and Manasseh is mine.
 Ephraim will produce my warriors,
 and Judah will produce my kings.
9 Moab will become my lowly servant,
 and Edom will be my slave.
 I will shout in triumph over the Philistines."

10 But who will bring me into the fortified city?
 Who will bring me victory over Edom?
11 Have you rejected us, O God?
 Will you no longer march with our armies?

12 Oh, please help us against
 our enemies,
 for all human help is useless.
13 With God's help we will do
 mighty things,
 for he will trample down our foes.

## PSALM 109

*For the choir director: A psalm of David.*

1 O God, whom I praise,
 don't stand silent and aloof
2 while the wicked slander me
 and tell lies about me.
3 They are all around me with their hateful words,
 and they fight against me for no reason.
4 I love them, but they try to destroy me—
 even as I am praying for them!
5 They return evil for good,
 and hatred for my love.

6 Arrange for an evil person to turn on him.
 Send an accuser to bring him to trial.
7 When his case is called for judgment,
 let him be pronounced guilty.
 Count his prayers as sins.
8 Let his years be few;
 let his position be given to someone else.
9 May his children become fatherless,
 and may his wife become a widow.
10 May his children wander as beggars;
 may they be evicted from their ruined homes.
11 May creditors seize his entire estate,
 and strangers take all he has earned.
12 Let no one be kind to him;
 let no one pity his fatherless children.
13 May all his offspring die.
 May his family name be blotted out in a
 single generation.
14 May the LORD never forget the sins of his
 ancestors;
 may his mother's sins never be erased from
 the record.
15 May these sins always remain before the LORD,
 but may his name be cut off from human
 memory.

**108:7** Or *in his sanctuary.*

16 For he refused all kindness to others;
　　he persecuted the poor and needy,
　　and he hounded the brokenhearted to death.
17 He loved to curse others;
　　now you curse him.
　He never blessed others;
　　now don't you bless him.
18 Cursing is as much a part of him as his clothing,
　　or as the water he drinks,
　　or the rich food he eats.
19 Now may his curses return and cling to him
　　like clothing;
　　may they be tied around him like a belt.

20 May those curses become the LORD's
　　punishment for my accusers
　　who are plotting against my life.
21 But deal well with me, O Sovereign LORD,
　　for the sake of your own reputation!
　Rescue me because you are so faithful and good.
22 　For I am poor and needy,
　　and my heart is full of pain.
23 I am fading like a shadow at dusk;
　　I am falling like a grasshopper that is brushed
　　aside.
24 My knees are weak from fasting,
　　and I am skin and bones.
25 I am an object of mockery to people
　　everywhere;
　　when they see me, they shake their heads.

26 Help me, O LORD my God!
　　Save me because of your unfailing love.
27 Let them see that this is your doing,
　　that you yourself have done it, LORD.
28 Then let them curse me if they like,
　　but you will bless me!
　When they attack me, they will be disgraced!
　　But I, your servant, will go right on rejoicing!
29 Make their humiliation obvious to all;
　　clothe my accusers with disgrace.
30 But I will give repeated thanks to the LORD,
　　praising him to everyone.
31 For he stands beside the needy,
　　ready to save them from those who condemn
　　them.

**110:2** Hebrew *Zion.*

## PSALM 110
*A psalm of David.*

1 The LORD said to my Lord,
　　"Sit in honor at my right hand
　until I humble your enemies,
　　making them a footstool under your
　　feet."

2 The LORD will extend your powerful
　　dominion from Jerusalem*;
　　you will rule over your enemies.
3 In that day of battle,
　　your people will serve you willingly.
　Arrayed in holy garments,
　　your vigor will be renewed each day like
　　the morning dew.
4 The LORD has taken an oath and will not
　　break his vow:
　　"You are a priest forever in the line of
　　Melchizedek."
5 The Lord stands at your right hand to protect
　　you.
　He will strike down many kings in the day
　　of his anger.
6 He will punish the nations
　　and fill them with their dead;
　he will shatter heads
　　over the whole earth.
7 But he himself will be refreshed from brooks
　　along the way.
　He will be victorious.

## PSALM 111
1 Praise the LORD!

　I will thank the LORD with all my heart
　　as I meet with his godly people.
2 How amazing are the deeds of the LORD!
　　All who delight in him should ponder
　　them.
3 Everything he does reveals his glory and
　　majesty.
　His righteousness never fails.
4 Who can forget the wonders he performs?
　　How gracious and merciful is our LORD!

5 He gives food to those
who trust him;
he always remembers his covenant.
6 He has shown his great power
to his people
by giving them the lands of other nations.
7 All he does is just and good,
and all his commandments are trustworthy.
8 They are forever true,
to be obeyed faithfully and with integrity.
9 He has paid a full ransom for his people.
He has guaranteed his covenant with them
forever.
What a holy, awe-inspiring name he has!
10 Reverence for the LORD is the foundation
of true wisdom.
The rewards of wisdom come to all who
obey him.

Praise his name forever!

## PSALM 112

1 Praise the LORD!

Happy are those who fear the LORD.
Yes, happy are those who delight in doing
what he commands.
2 Their children will be successful everywhere;
an entire generation of godly people will
be blessed.
3 They themselves will be wealthy,
and their good deeds will never be
forgotten.
4 When darkness overtakes the godly, light will
come bursting in.
They are* generous, compassionate, and
righteous.
5 All goes well for those who are generous,
who lend freely and conduct their business
fairly.
6 Such people will not be overcome by evil
circumstances.
Those who are righteous will be long
remembered.

112:4 Greek version reads *The LORD is.*

7 They do not fear bad news;
they confidently trust the LORD to care
for them.
8 They are confident and fearless
and can face their foes triumphantly.
9 They give generously to those in need.
Their good deeds will never be forgotten.
They will have influence and honor.
10 The wicked will be infuriated when they
see this.
They will grind their teeth in anger;
they will slink away, their hopes thwarted.

## PSALM 113

1 Praise the LORD!

Yes, give praise, O servants of the LORD.
Praise the name of the LORD!
2 Blessed be the name of the LORD
forever and ever.
3 Everywhere—from east to west—
praise the name of the LORD.
4 For the LORD is high above the nations;
his glory is far greater than the heavens.

5 Who can be compared with the LORD
our God,
who is enthroned on high?
6 Far below him are the heavens and the earth.
He stoops to look,
7 and he lifts the poor from the dirt
and the needy from the garbage dump.
8 He sets them among princes,
even the princes of his own people!
9 He gives the barren woman a home,
so that she becomes a happy mother.

Praise the LORD!

🖋 PSALM 112:1-2, 5, 7 Delighting in doing what God
commands comes from knowing that God's instructions
are good for us. Generosity and fairness are healthy! The
optimism in this psalm reminds us that the Lord's followers
ought to be happy people. One of the advantages of
being parents of young adults is that my wife and I can
see these promises fulfilled in our children as they mature.

Happy are those
who delight in doing
what he commands

Their children will be
successful everywhere *everywhere*
*everywhere* everywhere
e v e r y w h e r e

An entire generation of
godly people will be blessed
All goes well for
those who are GENEROUS
who lend freely and
conduct their business fairly
They do not fear bad news
They confidently
Trust the Lord
to care for them.

## PSALM 114

¹When the Israelites escaped from Egypt—
  when the family of Jacob left that foreign
    land—
²the land of Judah became God's sanctuary,
  and Israel became his kingdom.

³The Red Sea* saw them coming and hurried
    out of their way!
  The water of the Jordan River turned away.
⁴The mountains skipped like rams,
  the little hills like lambs!
⁵What's wrong, Red Sea, that made you hurry
    out of their way?
  What happened, Jordan River, that you
    turned away?
⁶Why, mountains, did you skip like rams?
  Why, little hills, like lambs?

⁷Tremble, O earth, at the presence of the Lord,
  at the presence of the God of Israel.*
⁸He turned the rock into pools of water;
  yes, springs of water came from solid rock.

## PSALM 115

¹Not to us, O LORD, but to you goes all the
    glory
  for your unfailing love and faithfulness.
²Why let the nations say,
  "Where is their God?"
³For our God is in the heavens,
  and he does as he wishes.
⁴Their idols are merely things of silver and gold,
  shaped by human hands.
⁵They cannot talk, though they have mouths,
  or see, though they have eyes!
⁶They cannot hear with their ears,
  or smell with their noses,
⁷  or feel with their hands,
  or walk with their feet,
  or utter sounds with their throats!
⁸And those who make them are just like them,
  as are all who trust in them.

⁹O Israel, trust the LORD!
  He is your helper; he is your shield.

¹⁰O priests of Aaron, trust the LORD!
  He is your helper; he is your shield.
¹¹All you who fear the LORD, trust the LORD!
  He is your helper; he is your shield.

¹²The LORD remembers us,
  and he will surely bless us.
  He will bless the people of Israel
    and the family of Aaron, the priests.
¹³He will bless those who fear the LORD,
  both great and small.

¹⁴May the LORD richly bless
  both you and your children.
¹⁵May you be blessed by the LORD,
  who made heaven and earth.
¹⁶The heavens belong to the LORD,
  but he has given the earth to all
    humanity.

¹⁷The dead cannot sing praises to the LORD,
  for they have gone into the silence of the
    grave.
¹⁸But we can praise the LORD
  both now and forever!

Praise the LORD!

## PSALM 116

¹I love the LORD because he hears
  and answers my prayers.
²Because he bends down and listens,
  I will pray as long as I have breath!
³Death had its hands around my throat;
  the terrors of the grave* overtook me.
  I saw only trouble and sorrow.
⁴Then I called on the name of the LORD:
  "Please, LORD, save me!"
⁵How kind the LORD is! How good he is!
  So merciful, this God of ours!
⁶The LORD protects those of childlike faith;
  I was facing death, and then he saved me.
⁷Now I can rest again,
  for the LORD has been so good to me.
⁸He has saved me from death,
  my eyes from tears,
  my feet from stumbling.

**114:3** Hebrew *the sea;* also in 114:5. **114:7** Hebrew *of Jacob.* **116:3** Hebrew *of Sheol.*

⁹And so I walk in the LORD's presence
   as I live here on earth!
¹⁰I believed in you, so I prayed,
   "I am deeply troubled, LORD."
¹¹In my anxiety I cried out to you,
   "These people are all liars!"
¹²What can I offer the LORD
   for all he has done for me?
¹³I will lift up a cup symbolizing his salvation;
   I will praise the LORD's name for saving me.
¹⁴I will keep my promises to the LORD
   in the presence of all his people.

¹⁵The LORD's loved ones are precious to him;
   it grieves him when they die.
¹⁶O LORD, I am your servant;
   yes, I am your servant, the son of your
      handmaid,
   and you have freed me from my bonds!
¹⁷I will offer you a sacrifice of thanksgiving
   and call on the name of the LORD.
¹⁸I will keep my promises to the LORD
   in the presence of all his people,
¹⁹in the house of the LORD,
   in the heart of Jerusalem.

   Praise the LORD!

## PSALM 117

¹Praise the LORD, all you nations.
   Praise him, all you people of the earth.
²For he loves us with unfailing love;
   the faithfulness of the LORD endures
      forever.

   Praise the LORD!

## PSALM 118

¹Give thanks to the LORD, for he is good!
   His faithful love endures forever.

²Let the congregation of Israel repeat:
   "His faithful love endures forever."
³Let Aaron's descendants, the priests, repeat:
   "His faithful love endures forever."
⁴Let all who fear the LORD repeat:
   "His faithful love endures forever."

PSALM 113:7, 9   I chose this special paper, hand-made from scraps, because it symbolizes that the Lord is in the business of refining us. Verses 5 and 6 speak of God's lofty position, which makes these verses all the more remarkable. The words in the second part of this text echo those of Hannah, who became the mother of the great prophet Samuel.

⁵In my distress I prayed to the LORD,
   and the LORD answered me and
      rescued me.

6 The LORD is for me, so I will not be afraid.
  What can mere mortals do to me?
7 Yes, the LORD is for me; he will help me.
  I will look in triumph at those who hate me.
8 It is better to trust the LORD
  than to put confidence in people.
9 It is better to trust the LORD
  than to put confidence in princes.

10 Though hostile nations surrounded me,
  I destroyed them all in the name of the
  LORD.
11 Yes, they surrounded and attacked me,
  but I destroyed them all in the name of the
  LORD.
12 They swarmed around me like bees;
  they blazed against me like a roaring flame.
  But I destroyed them all in the name of the
  LORD.
13 You did your best to kill me, O my enemy,
  but the LORD helped me.
14 The LORD is my strength and my song;
  he has become my victory.
15 Songs of joy and victory are sung in the camp
  of the godly.
  The strong right arm of the LORD has done
  glorious things!
16 The strong right arm of the LORD is raised in
  triumph.
  The strong right arm of the LORD has done
  glorious things!
17 I will not die, but I will live
  to tell what the LORD has done.
18 The LORD has punished me severely,
  but he has not handed me over to death.

19 Open for me the gates where the righteous
  enter,
  and I will go in and thank the LORD.
20 Those gates lead to the presence of the LORD,
  and the godly enter there.
21 I thank you for answering my prayer
  and saving me!

22 The stone rejected by the builders
  has now become the cornerstone.

23 This is the LORD's doing,
  and it is marvelous to see.
24 This is the day the LORD has made.
  We will rejoice and be glad in it.
25 Please, LORD, please save us.
  Please, LORD, please give us success.
26 Bless the one who comes in the name of the
  LORD.
  We bless you from the house of the LORD.
27 The LORD is God, shining upon us.
  Bring forward the sacrifice and put it on the
  altar.
28 You are my God, and I will praise you!
  You are my God, and I will exalt you!

29 Give thanks to the LORD, for he is good!
  His faithful love endures forever.

## PSALM 119

1 Happy are people of integrity,
  who follow the law of the LORD.
2 Happy are those who obey his decrees
  and search for him with all their hearts.
3 They do not compromise with evil,
  and they walk only in his paths.
4 You have charged us
  to keep your commandments carefully.
5 Oh, that my actions would consistently
  reflect your principles!
6 Then I will not be disgraced
  when I compare my life with your
  commands.
7 When I learn your righteous laws,
  I will thank you by living as I should!
8 I will obey your principles.
  Please don't give up on me!

9 How can a young person stay pure?
  By obeying your word and following its
  rules.

🖋 PSALM 116:1-2, 6, 15  Those who pray see God work. The heart of God comes through here—he bends down to listen and he grieves our death. I tried to capture this intimacy by bending all the phrases into one another.

---

**119** This psalm is a Hebrew acrostic poem; there are 22 stanzas, one for each letter of the Hebrew alphabet. The 8 verses within each stanza begin with the Hebrew letter of its section.

I love the LORD
because he hears

and answers my prayers

Because he bends down
and listens,

I will pray
I will pray as I have breath
as long as I have breath
as long as I have breath

The LORD protects
those of childlike faith

The LORD's loved ones are precious to him

It grieves him when they die

¹⁰I have tried my best to find you—
    don't let me wander from your commands.
¹¹I have hidden your word in my heart,
    that I might not sin against you.
¹²Blessed are you, O LORD;
    teach me your principles.
¹³I have recited aloud
    all the laws you have given us.
¹⁴I have rejoiced in your decrees
    as much as in riches.
¹⁵I will study your commandments
    and reflect on your ways.
¹⁶I will delight in your principles
    and not forget your word.

¹⁷Be good to your servant,
    that I may live and obey your word.
¹⁸Open my eyes to see
    the wonderful truths in your law.
¹⁹I am but a foreigner here on earth;
    I need the guidance of your commands.
    Don't hide them from me!
²⁰I am overwhelmed continually
    with a desire for your laws.
²¹You rebuke those cursed proud ones
    who wander from your commands.
²²Don't let them scorn and insult me,
    for I have obeyed your decrees.
²³Even princes sit and speak against me,
    but I will meditate on your principles.
²⁴Your decrees please me;
    they give me wise advice.

²⁵I lie in the dust, completely discouraged;
    revive me by your word.
²⁶I told you my plans, and you answered.
    Now teach me your principles.
²⁷Help me understand the meaning of your
        commandments,
    and I will meditate on your wonderful
        miracles.
²⁸I weep with grief;
    encourage me by your word.
²⁹Keep me from lying to myself;
    give me the privilege of knowing your
        law.

³⁰I have chosen to be faithful;
    I have determined to live by your laws.
³¹I cling to your decrees.
    LORD, don't let me be put to shame!
³²If you will help me,
    I will run to follow your commands.

³³Teach me, O LORD,
    to follow every one of your principles.
³⁴Give me understanding and I will obey your
        law;
    I will put it into practice with all my
        heart.
³⁵Make me walk along the path of your
        commands,
    for that is where my happiness is found.
³⁶Give me an eagerness for your decrees;
    do not inflict me with love for money!
³⁷Turn my eyes from worthless things,
    and give me life through your word.*
³⁸Reassure me of your promise,
    which is for those who honor you.
³⁹Help me abandon my shameful ways;
    your laws are all I want in life.
⁴⁰I long to obey your commandments!
    Renew my life with your goodness.

⁴¹LORD, give to me your unfailing love,
    the salvation that you promised me.
⁴²Then I will have an answer for those who
        taunt me,
    for I trust in your word.
⁴³Do not snatch your word of truth from me,
    for my only hope is in your laws.
⁴⁴I will keep on obeying your law
    forever and forever.
⁴⁵I will walk in freedom,
    for I have devoted myself to your
        commandments.

✎ PSALM 119:11, 18, 105, 162, 165   This piece is
inspired by Chaim Potok's passionate description of
dancing with the Torah scroll in *The Gift of Asher Lev.*
It is a beautiful picture of how deeply we should
embrace God's teachings. But sometimes we need
God to unlock the secrets of his Word, because we
are blinded by errors that filter in from all directions.

**119:37** Some manuscripts read *in your ways.*

# Open my eyes

to see the wonderful truths in your law

Your word is a lamp for my feet and a light for my path

I have hidden your word in my heart that I might not sin against you

I rejoice in your word like one who finds a great treasure

Those who love your law have great peace and do not stumble

⁴⁶I will speak to kings about your decrees,
and I will not be ashamed.
⁴⁷How I delight in your commands!
How I love them!
⁴⁸I honor and love your commands.
I meditate on your principles.

⁴⁹Remember your promise to me,
for it is my only hope.
⁵⁰Your promise revives me;
it comforts me in all my troubles.
⁵¹The proud hold me in utter contempt,
but I do not turn away from your law.
⁵²I meditate on your age-old laws;
O LORD, they comfort me.
⁵³I am furious with the wicked,
those who reject your law.
⁵⁴Your principles have been the music of my life
throughout the years of my pilgrimage.
⁵⁵I reflect at night on who you are, O LORD,
and I obey your law because of this.
⁵⁶This is my happy way of life:
obeying your commandments.

⁵⁷LORD, you are mine!
I promise to obey your words!
⁵⁸With all my heart I want your blessings.
Be merciful just as you promised.
⁵⁹I pondered the direction of my life,
and I turned to follow your statutes.
⁶⁰I will hurry, without lingering,
to obey your commands.
⁶¹Evil people try to drag me into sin,
but I am firmly anchored to your law.
⁶²At midnight I rise to thank you
for your just laws.
⁶³Anyone who fears you is my friend—
anyone who obeys your commandments.
⁶⁴O LORD, the earth is full of your unfailing
love;
teach me your principles.

⁶⁵You have done many good things for me,
LORD,
just as you promised.
⁶⁶I believe in your commands;
now teach me good judgment and
knowledge.

⁶⁷I used to wander off until you disciplined me;
but now I closely follow your word.
⁶⁸You are good and do only good;
teach me your principles.
⁶⁹Arrogant people have made up lies about me,
but in truth I obey your commandments
with all my heart.
⁷⁰Their hearts are dull and stupid,
but I delight in your law.
⁷¹The suffering you sent was good for me,
for it taught me to pay attention to your
principles.
⁷²Your law is more valuable to me
than millions in gold and silver!

⁷³You made me; you created me.
Now give me the sense to follow your
commands.
⁷⁴May all who fear you find in me a cause
for joy,
for I have put my hope in your word.
⁷⁵I know, O LORD, that your decisions are fair;
you disciplined me because I needed it.
⁷⁶Now let your unfailing love comfort me,
just as you promised me, your servant.
⁷⁷Surround me with your tender mercies so
I may live,
for your law is my delight.
⁷⁸Bring disgrace upon the arrogant people who
lied about me;
meanwhile, I will concentrate on your
commandments.
⁷⁹Let me be reconciled
with all who fear you and know your
decrees.
⁸⁰May I be blameless in keeping your principles;
then I will never have to be ashamed.

⁸¹I faint with longing for your salvation;
but I have put my hope in your word.
⁸²My eyes are straining to see your promises
come true.
When will you comfort me?
⁸³I am shriveled like a wineskin in the smoke,
exhausted with waiting.
But I cling to your principles and obey
them.

84 How long must I wait?
  When will you punish those who persecute me?
85 These arrogant people who hate your law
  have dug deep pits for me to fall into.
86 All your commands are trustworthy.
  Protect me from those who hunt me down
    without cause.
87 They almost finished me off,
  but I refused to abandon your
    commandments.
88 In your unfailing love, spare my life;
  then I can continue to obey your decrees.

89 Forever, O LORD,
  your word stands firm in heaven.
90 Your faithfulness extends to every generation,
  as enduring as the earth you created.
91 Your laws remain true today,
  for everything serves your plans.
92 If your law hadn't sustained me with joy,
  I would have died in my misery.
93 I will never forget your commandments,
  for you have used them to restore my joy
    and health.
94 I am yours; save me!
  For I have applied myself to obey your
    commandments.
95 Though the wicked hide along the way to
    kill me,
  I will quietly keep my mind on your
    decrees.
96 Even perfection has its limits,
  but your commands have no limit.

97 Oh, how I love your law!
  I think about it all day long.
98 Your commands make me wiser than my
    enemies,
  for your commands are my constant guide.
99 Yes, I have more insight than my teachers,
  for I am always thinking of your decrees.
100 I am even wiser than my elders,
  for I have kept your commandments.
101 I have refused to walk on any path of evil,
  that I may remain obedient to your word.
102 I haven't turned away from your laws,
  for you have taught me well.

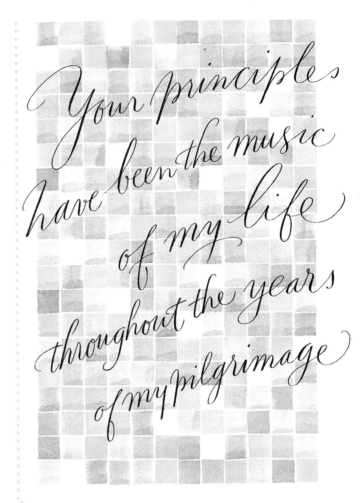

*Your principles have been the music of my life throughout the years of my pilgrimage*

✎ PSALM 119:54   God's laws have brought the theme of joy to my life—the source for my smile, the spring in my step, the energy behind my work. The squares of color here represent the days of our life. Some are bright and some are dreary, but together they make a rich tapestry. I combined a spontaneous, personal style of handwriting with the discipline of a nineteenth century writing instrument for this piece.

103 How sweet are your words to my taste;
  they are sweeter than honey.
104 Your commandments give me under-
    standing;
  no wonder I hate every false way of life.

105 Your word is a lamp for my feet
  and a light for my path.
106 I've promised it once, and I'll promise again:
  I will obey your wonderful laws.
107 I have suffered much, O LORD;
  restore my life again, just as you promised.

108 LORD, accept my grateful thanks
  and teach me your laws.
109 My life constantly hangs in the balance,
  but I will not stop obeying your law.
110 The wicked have set their traps for me along
    your path,
  but I will not turn from your
    commandments.
111 Your decrees are my treasure;
  they are truly my heart's delight.
112 I am determined to keep your principles,
  even forever, to the very end.

113 I hate those who are undecided about you,
  but my choice is clear—I love your law.
114 You are my refuge and my shield;
  your word is my only source of hope.
115 Get out of my life, you evil-minded people,
  for I intend to obey the commands of my
    God.
116 LORD, sustain me as you promised, that I may
    live!
  Do not let my hope be crushed.
117 Sustain me, and I will be saved;
  then I will meditate on your principles
    continually.
118 But you have rejected all who stray from your
    principles.
  They are only fooling themselves.
119 All the wicked of the earth are the scum you
    skim off;
  no wonder I love to obey your decrees!
120 I tremble in fear of you;
  I fear your judgments.

121 Don't leave me to the mercy of my enemies,
  for I have done what is just and right.
122 Please guarantee a blessing for me.
  Don't let those who are arrogant oppress
    me!
123 My eyes strain to see your deliverance,
  to see the truth of your promise fulfilled.
124 I am your servant;
  deal with me in unfailing love,
  and teach me your principles.
125 Give discernment to me, your servant;
  then I will understand your decrees.

126 LORD, it is time for you to act,
  for these evil people have
    broken your law.
127 Truly, I love your commands
  more than gold, even the finest
    gold.
128 Truly, each of your commandments
  is right.
  That is why I hate every false way.

129 Your decrees are wonderful.
  No wonder I obey them!
130 As your words are taught, they give light;
  even the simple can understand them.
131 I open my mouth, panting expectantly,
  longing for your commands.
132 Come and show me your mercy,
  as you do for all who love your name.
133 Guide my steps by your word,
  so I will not be overcome by any evil.
134 Rescue me from the oppression of evil
    people;
  then I can obey your commandments.
135 Look down on me with love;
  teach me all your principles.
136 Rivers of tears gush from my eyes
  because people disobey your law.

137 O LORD, you are righteous,
  and your decisions are fair.
138 Your decrees are perfect;
  they are entirely worthy of our trust.
139 I am overwhelmed with rage,
  for my enemies have disregarded your
    words.
140 Your promises have been thoroughly tested;
  that is why I love them so much.
141 I am insignificant and despised,
  but I don't forget your commandments.
142 Your justice is eternal,
  and your law is perfectly true.
143 As pressure and stress bear down on me,
  I find joy in your commands.
144 Your decrees are always fair;
  help me to understand them, that I may live.
145 I pray with all my heart; answer me, LORD!
  I will obey your principles.

146 I cry out to you; save me,
    that I may obey your decrees.
147 I rise early, before the sun is up;
    I cry out for help and put my hope in your
        words.
148 I stay awake through the night,
    thinking about your promise.
149 In your faithful love, O LORD, hear my cry;
    in your justice, save my life.
150 Those lawless people are coming near to
        attack me;
    they live far from your law.
151 But you are near, O LORD,
    and all your commands are true.
152 I have known from my earliest days
    that your decrees never change.

153 Look down upon my sorrows and rescue me,
    for I have not forgotten your law.
154 Argue my case; take my side!
    Protect my life as you promised.
155 The wicked are far from salvation,
    for they do not bother with your principles.
156 LORD, how great is your mercy;
    in your justice, give me back my life.
157 Many persecute and trouble me,
    yet I have not swerved from your decrees.
158 I hate these traitors
    because they care nothing for your word.
159 See how I love your commandments, LORD.
    Give back my life because of your unfailing
        love.
160 All your words are true;
    all your just laws will stand forever.

161 Powerful people harass me without cause,
    but my heart trembles only at your word.
162 I rejoice in your word
    like one who finds a great treasure.
163 I hate and abhor all falsehood,
    but I love your law.
164 I will praise you seven times a day
    because all your laws are just.
165 Those who love your law have great peace
    and do not stumble.
166 I long for your salvation, LORD,
    so I have obeyed your commands.

167 I have obeyed your decrees,
    and I love them very much.
168 Yes, I obey your commandments and
        decrees,
    because you know everything I do.

169 O LORD, listen to my cry;
    give me the discerning mind you promised.
170 Listen to my prayer;
    rescue me as you promised.
171 Let my lips burst forth with praise,
    for you have taught me your principles.
172 Let my tongue sing about your word,
    for all your commands are right.
173 Stand ready to help me,
    for I have chosen to follow your
        commandments.
174 O LORD, I have longed for your salvation,
    and your law is my delight.
175 Let me live so I can praise you,
    and may your laws sustain me.
176 I have wandered away like a lost sheep;
    come and find me,
    for I have not forgotten your commands.

## PSALM 120

*A song for the ascent to Jerusalem.*

1 I took my troubles to the LORD;
    I cried out to him, and he answered my
        prayer.
2 Rescue me, O LORD, from liars
    and from all deceitful people.
3 O deceptive tongue, what will God do
        to you?
    How will he increase your punishment?
4 You will be pierced with sharp arrows
    and burned with glowing coals.

5 How I suffer among these scoundrels of
        Meshech!
    It pains me to live with these people from
        Kedar!
6 I am tired of living here
    among people who hate peace.
7 As for me, I am for peace;
    but when I speak, they are for war!

## PSALM 121

*A song for the ascent to Jerusalem.*

¹I look up to the mountains—
  does my help come from there?
²My help comes from the LORD,
  who made the heavens and the earth!

³He will not let you stumble and fall;
  the one who watches over you will not
    sleep.
⁴Indeed, he who watches over Israel
  never tires and never sleeps.

⁵The LORD himself watches over you!
  The LORD stands beside you as your
    protective shade.
⁶The sun will not hurt you by day,
  nor the moon at night.
⁷The LORD keeps you from all evil
  and preserves your life.
⁸The LORD keeps watch over you as you
    come and go,
  both now and forever.

## PSALM 122

*A song for the ascent to Jerusalem. A psalm of David.*

¹I was glad when they said to me,
  "Let us go to the house of the LORD."
²And now we are standing here
  inside your gates, O Jerusalem.
³Jerusalem is a well-built city,
  knit together as a single unit.
⁴All the people of Israel—the LORD's people—
  make their pilgrimage here.
  They come to give thanks to the name
    of the LORD
  as the law requires.
⁵Here stand the thrones where judgment is
    given,
  the thrones of the dynasty of David.

⁶Pray for the peace of Jerusalem.
  May all who love this city prosper.
⁷O Jerusalem, may there be peace within your
    walls
  and prosperity in your palaces.

⁸For the sake of my family and friends,
    I will say,
  "Peace be with you."
⁹For the sake of the house of the LORD
    our God,
  I will seek what is best for you, O Jerusalem.

## PSALM 123

*A song for the ascent to Jerusalem.*

¹I lift my eyes to you,
  O God, enthroned in heaven.
²We look to the LORD our God for his mercy,
  just as servants keep their eyes on their
    master,
  as a slave girl watches her mistress for the
    slightest signal.

³Have mercy on us, LORD, have mercy,
  for we have had our fill of contempt.
⁴We have had our fill of the scoffing of the
    proud
  and the contempt of the arrogant.

## PSALM 124

*A song for the ascent to Jerusalem. A psalm of David.*

¹If the LORD had not been on our side—
  let Israel now say—
²if the LORD had not been on our side
  when people rose up against us,
³they would have swallowed us alive
  because of their burning anger against us.
⁴The waters would have engulfed us;
  a torrent would have overwhelmed us.
⁵Yes, the raging waters of their fury
  would have overwhelmed our very lives.

⁶Blessed be the LORD,
  who did not let their teeth tear us apart!

✎ PSALM 121:1-3 Icons or symbols are useful to help us worship the Lord. They picture for us what we cannot see. Images become dangerous only when we begin to worship them. Having lived in Japan for three years, I have powerful memories of waking up to a view of Mt. Fuji towering over Tokyo. But if you climb it, you'll find nothing but barrenness. The greater glory is still higher.

I look up
to the
mountains-
Does my help
come from
there?
My help
comes
from the
LORD
who made
the heavens
and the
earth!
The one who
watches
over you
will not
sleep

7 We escaped like a bird from a hunter's trap.
    The trap is broken, and we are free!
8 Our help is from the LORD,
    who made the heavens and the earth.

## PSALM 125

*A song for the ascent to Jerusalem.*

1 Those who trust in the LORD are as secure
        as Mount Zion;
    they will not be defeated but will endure
        forever.
2 Just as the mountains surround and protect
        Jerusalem,
    so the LORD surrounds and protects his
        people, both now and forever.
3 The wicked will not rule the godly,
    for then the godly might be forced to do
        wrong.
4 O LORD, do good to those who are good,
    whose hearts are in tune with you.
5 But banish those who turn to crooked ways,
        O LORD.
    Take them away with those who do evil.
    And let Israel have quietness and peace.

## PSALM 126

*A song for the ascent to Jerusalem.*

1 When the LORD restored his exiles to
        Jerusalem,*
    it was like a dream!
2 We were filled with laughter,
    and we sang for joy.
    And the other nations said,
    "What amazing things the LORD has done
        for them."
3 Yes, the LORD has done amazing things for us!
    What joy!

4 Restore our fortunes, LORD,
    as streams renew the desert.
5 Those who plant in tears
    will harvest with shouts of joy.
6 They weep as they go to plant their seed,
    but they sing as they return with the harvest.

126:1 Hebrew *Zion.*

## PSALM 127

*A song for the ascent to Jerusalem. A psalm of Solomon.*

1 Unless the LORD builds a house,
    the work of the builders is useless.
    Unless the LORD protects a city,
        guarding it with sentries will do no good.
2 It is useless for you to work so hard
    from early morning until late at night,
    anxiously working for food to eat;
    for God gives rest to his loved ones.

3 Children are a gift from the LORD;
    they are a reward from him.
4 Children born to a young man
    are like sharp arrows in a warrior's
        hands.
5 How happy is the man whose quiver is full
        of them!
    He will not be put to shame when he
        confronts his accusers at the city gates.

## PSALM 128

*A song for the ascent to Jerusalem.*

1 How happy are those who fear the LORD—
    all who follow his ways!
2 You will enjoy the fruit of your labor.
    How happy you will be! How rich your
        life!
3 Your wife will be like a fruitful vine,
    flourishing within your home.
    And look at all those children!
    There they sit around your table
    as vigorous and healthy as young olive trees.
4 That is the LORD's reward
    for those who fear him.

5 May the LORD continually bless you from
        Zion.

PSALM 122:6-7, 9   We should care about the
welfare of Jerusalem because God's blessing is upon
her to cause her to succeed. If we tamper with Jerusalem, we tangle with the Almighty! I chose to work the
pomegranate into this design because it is specifically
mentioned as an element in the decoration of Solomon's temple and is symbolic of fruitfulness.

PRAY FOR THE PEACE OF JERUSALEM
MAY ALL WHO LOVE THIS CITY PROSPER
O JERUSALEM, MAY THERE BE PEACE
WITHIN YOUR WALLS
AND PROSPERITY IN YOUR PALACES
FOR THE SAKE OF THE HOUSE
OF THE LORD OUR GOD
I WILL SEEK WHAT IS BEST FOR YOU
O JERUSALEM

PSALM 1 2 9

May you see Jerusalem prosper as long as
you live.
⁶May you live to enjoy your grandchildren.
And may Israel have quietness and peace.

## PSALM 129

*A song for the ascent to Jerusalem.*

¹From my earliest youth my enemies have
persecuted me—
let Israel now say—
²from my earliest youth my enemies have
persecuted me,
but they have never been able to finish
me off.
³My back is covered with cuts,
as if a farmer had plowed long furrows.
⁴But the LORD is good;
he has cut the cords used by the ungodly to
bind me.

⁵May all who hate Jerusalem*
be turned back in shameful defeat.
⁶May they be as useless as grass on a rooftop,
turning yellow when only half grown,
⁷ ignored by the harvester,
despised by the binder.
⁸And may those who pass by refuse to give
them this blessing:
"The LORD's blessings be upon you;
we bless you in the LORD's name."

## PSALM 130

*A song for the ascent to Jerusalem.*

¹From the depths of despair, O LORD,
I call for your help.
²Hear my cry, O Lord.
Pay attention to my prayer.

³LORD, if you kept a record of our sins,
who, O Lord, could ever survive?
⁴But you offer forgiveness,
that we might learn to fear you.

⁵I am counting on the LORD;
yes, I am counting on him.
I have put my hope in his word.

⁶I long for the Lord
more than sentries long for the dawn,
yes, more than sentries long for the dawn.

⁷O Israel, hope in the LORD;
for with the LORD there is unfailing love
and an overflowing supply of salvation.
⁸He himself will free Israel
from every kind of sin.

## PSALM 131

*A song for the ascent to Jerusalem. A psalm of David.*

¹LORD, my heart is not proud;
my eyes are not haughty.
I don't concern myself with matters too great
or awesome for me.
²But I have stilled and quieted myself,
just as a small child is quiet with its mother.
Yes, like a small child is my soul within me.

³O Israel, put your hope in the LORD—
now and always.

## PSALM 132

*A song for the ascent to Jerusalem.*

¹LORD, remember David
and all that he suffered.
²He took an oath before the LORD.
He vowed to the Mighty One of Israel,*
³"I will not go home;
I will not let myself rest.
⁴I will not let my eyes sleep
nor close my eyelids in slumber
⁵ until I find a place to build a house for the
LORD,
a sanctuary for the Mighty One of Israel."
⁶We heard that the Ark was in Ephrathah;
then we found it in the distant countryside
of Jaar.

PSALM 127  Trying to build our home without
the Lord as its foundation is to miss the spiritual dimension. All work and no praying depletes our energy. An
older friend of ours doesn't have children of her own,
but she has taken on others' children to nurture. Her
life is full of zest because they keep her looking toward
the future.

129:5 Hebrew *Zion*.  132:2 Hebrew *of Jacob;* also in 132:5.

11    Sihon king of the Amorites,
      Og king of Bashan,
      and all the kings of Canaan.
12 He gave their land as an inheritance,
      a special possession to his people Israel.
13 Your name, O LORD, endures forever;
      your fame, O LORD, is known to every
      generation.
14 For the LORD will vindicate his people
      and have compassion on his servants.

15 Their idols are merely things of silver and
      gold,
      shaped by human hands.
16 They cannot talk, though they have mouths,
      or see, though they have eyes!
17 They cannot hear with their ears
      or smell with their noses.
18 And those who make them are just like them,
      as are all who trust in them.

19 O Israel, praise the LORD!
      O priests of Aaron, praise the LORD!
20 O Levites, praise the LORD!
      All you who fear the LORD, praise the
      LORD!
21 The LORD be praised from Zion,
      for he lives here in Jerusalem.

      Praise the LORD!

## PSALM 136

1 Give thanks to the LORD, for he is good!
      *His faithful love endures forever.*
2 Give thanks to the God of gods.
      *His faithful love endures forever.*
3 Give thanks to the Lord of lords.
      *His faithful love endures forever.*

4 Give thanks to him who alone does mighty
      miracles.
      *His faithful love endures forever.*
5 Give thanks to him who made the heavens
      so skillfully.
      *His faithful love endures forever.*
6 Give thanks to him who placed the earth
      on the water.
      *His faithful love endures forever.*

PSALM 133:1   Peace should be celebrated and pursued. My friend Jack Strating writes: "Harmony is not the result of everyone singing the same note." There is beauty in diversity if blending takes place. We cannot act independently of each other but should rather act with regard for each other—as indicated here by the interconnected letters.

7 Give thanks to him who made the heavenly
      lights—
      *His faithful love endures forever.*
8   the sun to rule the day,
      *His faithful love endures forever.*
9   and the moon and stars to rule the night.
      *His faithful love endures forever.*

¹⁰Give thanks to him who killed the firstborn
of Egypt.
*His faithful love endures forever.*
¹¹He brought Israel out of Egypt.
*His faithful love endures forever.*
¹²He acted with a strong hand and powerful arm.
*His faithful love endures forever.*
¹³Give thanks to him who parted the Red Sea.⋆
*His faithful love endures forever.*
¹⁴He led Israel safely through,
*His faithful love endures forever.*
¹⁵ but he hurled Pharaoh and his army into
the sea.
*His faithful love endures forever.*
¹⁶Give thanks to him who led his people
through the wilderness.
*His faithful love endures forever.*

¹⁷Give thanks to him who struck down mighty
kings.
*His faithful love endures forever.*
¹⁸He killed powerful kings—
*His faithful love endures forever.*
¹⁹ Sihon king of the Amorites,
*His faithful love endures forever.*
²⁰ and Og king of Bashan.
*His faithful love endures forever.*
²¹God gave the land of these kings as an
inheritance—
*His faithful love endures forever.*
²² a special possession to his servant Israel.
*His faithful love endures forever.*

²³He remembered our utter weakness.
*His faithful love endures forever.*
²⁴He saved us from our enemies.
*His faithful love endures forever.*
²⁵He gives food to every living thing.
*His faithful love endures forever.*

²⁶Give thanks to the God of heaven.
*His faithful love endures forever.*

## PSALM 137

¹Beside the rivers of Babylon, we sat and wept
as we thought of Jerusalem.⋆

**136:13** Hebrew *sea of reeds;* also in 136:15. **137:1** Hebrew *Zion;* also in 137:3.

²We put away our lyres,
hanging them on the branches of the willow
trees.
³For there our captors demanded a song of us.
Our tormentors requested a joyful hymn:
"Sing us one of those songs of Jerusalem!"
⁴But how can we sing the songs of the LORD
while in a foreign land?

⁵If I forget you, O Jerusalem,
let my right hand forget its skill upon the
harp.
⁶May my tongue stick to the roof of my mouth
if I fail to remember you,
if I don't make Jerusalem my highest joy.

⁷O LORD, remember what the Edomites did
on the day the armies of Babylon captured
Jerusalem.
"Destroy it!" they yelled.
"Level it to the ground!"
⁸O Babylon, you will be destroyed.
Happy is the one who pays you back
for what you have done to us.
⁹Happy is the one who takes your babies
and smashes them against the rocks!

## PSALM 138

*A psalm of David.*

¹I give you thanks, O LORD, with all my heart;
I will sing your praises before the gods.
²I bow before your holy Temple as I worship.
I will give thanks to your name
for your unfailing love and faithfulness,
because your promises are backed
by all the honor of your name.
³When I pray, you answer me;
you encourage me by giving me the strength
I need.

✎ PSALM 139:7, 9-10 It is futile to try to escape
from God because he is omnipresent. It is better to
try to understand who he is. His is more than a spooky
presence; he desires to be with me as a traveling
companion. This explains the use of the compass and
its colorful emphasis.

I CAN NEVER ESCAPE
FROM YOUR SPIRIT
I CAN NEVER GET AWAY
FROM YOUR PRESENCE
IF I RIDE THE WINGS
OF THE MORNING
IF I DWELL BY THE FARTHEST OCEANS

EVEN THERE YOUR HAND WILL GUIDE ME
AND YOUR STRENGTH WILL SUPPORT ME

⁴Every king in all the earth will give you
    thanks, O LORD,
  for all of them will hear your words.
⁵Yes, they will sing about the LORD's ways,
  for the glory of the LORD is very great.
⁶Though the LORD is great, he cares for the
    humble,
  but he keeps his distance from the proud.

⁷Though I am surrounded by troubles,
  you will preserve me against the anger of my
    enemies.
  You will clench your fist against my angry
    enemies!
  Your power will save me.
⁸The LORD will work out his plans for my
    life—
  for your faithful love, O LORD, endures
    forever.
  Don't abandon me, for you made me.

## PSALM 139

*For the choir director: A psalm of David.*

¹O LORD, you have examined my heart
  and know everything about me.
²You know when I sit down or stand up.
  You know my every thought when far away.
³You chart the path ahead of me
  and tell me where to stop and rest.
  Every moment you know where I am.
⁴You know what I am going to say
  even before I say it, LORD.
⁵You both precede and follow me.
  You place your hand of blessing on my
    head.
⁶Such knowledge is too wonderful for me,
  too great for me to know!

⁷I can never escape from your spirit!
  I can never get away from your presence!
⁸If I go up to heaven, you are there;
  if I go down to the place of the dead,*
    you are there.
⁹If I ride the wings of the morning,
  if I dwell by the farthest oceans,

¹⁰even there your hand will guide me,
  and your strength will support me.
¹¹I could ask the darkness to hide me
  and the light around me to become night—
¹²  but even in darkness I cannot hide from you.
  To you the night shines as bright as day.
  Darkness and light are both alike to you.

¹³You made all the delicate, inner parts of my
    body
  and knit me together in my mother's womb.
¹⁴Thank you for making me so wonderfully
    complex!
  Your workmanship is marvelous—and how
    well I know it.
¹⁵You watched me as I was being formed in utter
    seclusion,
  as I was woven together in the dark of the
    womb.
¹⁶You saw me before I was born.
  Every day of my life was recorded in your
    book.
  Every moment was laid out
    before a single day had passed.

¹⁷How precious are your thoughts about me,*
    O God!
  They are innumerable!
¹⁸I can't even count them;
  they outnumber the grains of sand!
  And when I wake up in the morning,
    you are still with me!

¹⁹O God, if only you would destroy the wicked!
  Get out of my life, you murderers!
²⁰They blaspheme you;
  your enemies take your name in vain.
²¹O LORD, shouldn't I hate those who hate you?
  Shouldn't I despise those who resist you?
²²Yes, I hate them with complete hatred,
  for your enemies are my enemies.

✒ PSALM 139:1, 13-17   My self-image is boosted
by the knowledge that God made me with deliberate
intentions. Through ultrasound we can even catch a
glimpse of this mystery in process. This is one of three
pieces in this book collaborating with Charles and
Gretchen Peterson, who did the marbling.

**139:8** Hebrew *to Sheol.* **139:17** Or *How precious to me are your thoughts.*

O Lord you have examined my heart and know everything about me

You made all the delicate inner parts of my body
and knit me together in my mother's womb
Thank you for making me so wonderfully complex
Your workmanship is marvelous and how well I know it
You watched me as I was being formed in utter seclusion
as I was woven together in the dark of the womb
You saw me before I was born
Every day of my life was recorded in your book
How precious are your thoughts about me O God

23 Search me, O God, and know my heart;
    test me and know my thoughts.
24 Point out anything in me that offends you,
    and lead me along the path of everlasting life.

## PSALM 140

*For the choir director: A psalm of David.*

1 O LORD, rescue me from evil people.
    Preserve me from those who are violent,
2 those who plot evil in their hearts
    and stir up trouble all day long.
3 Their tongues sting like a snake;
    the poison of a viper drips from their lips.
        *Interlude*

4 O LORD, keep me out of the hands of the
    wicked.
    Preserve me from those who are violent,
    for they are plotting against me.
5 The proud have set a trap to catch me;
    they have stretched out a net;
    they have placed traps all along the way.
        *Interlude*

6 I said to the LORD, "You are my God!"
    Listen, O LORD, to my cries for mercy!
7 O Sovereign LORD, my strong savior,
    you protected me on the day of battle.
8 LORD, do not give in to their evil desires.
    Do not let their evil schemes succeed,
        O God.    *Interlude*

9 Let my enemies be destroyed
    by the very evil they have planned for me.
10 Let burning coals fall down on their heads,
    or throw them into the fire,
    or into deep pits from which they can't
    escape.
11 Don't let liars prosper here in our land.
    Cause disaster to fall with great force on the
    violent.

12 But I know the LORD will surely help those
    they persecute;
    he will maintain the rights of the poor.
13 Surely the godly are praising your name,
    for they will live in your presence.

## PSALM 141

*A psalm of David.*

1 O LORD, I am calling to you. Please hurry!
    Listen when I cry to you for help!
2 Accept my prayer as incense offered to you,
    and my upraised hands as an evening
    offering.

3 Take control of what I say, O LORD,
    and keep my lips sealed.
4 Don't let me lust for evil things;
    don't let me participate in acts of
    wickedness.
    Don't let me share in the delicacies
    of those who do evil.

5 Let the godly strike me!
    It will be a kindness!
    If they reprove me, it is soothing medicine.
    Don't let me refuse it.

    But I am in constant prayer
    against the wicked and their deeds.
6 When their leaders are thrown down from a
    cliff,
    they will listen to my words and find them
    pleasing.
7 Even as a farmer breaks up the soil and brings
    up rocks,
    so the bones of the wicked will be scattered
    without a decent burial.

8 I look to you for help, O Sovereign LORD.
    You are my refuge; don't let them kill me.
9 Keep me out of the traps they have set
    for me,
    out of the snares of those who do evil.
10 Let the wicked fall into their own snares,
    but let me escape.

## PSALM 142

*A psalm of David, regarding his experience in the cave.
A prayer.*

1 I cry out to the LORD;
    I plead for the LORD's mercy.
2 I pour out my complaints before him
    and tell him all my troubles.

³For I am overwhelmed,
 and you alone know the way I should
  turn.
Wherever I go,
 my enemies have set traps for me.
⁴I look for someone to come and help me,
 but no one gives me a passing thought!
No one will help me;
 no one cares a bit what happens to me.
⁵Then I pray to you, O LORD.
 I say, "You are my place of refuge.
 You are all I really want in life.
⁶Hear my cry,
 for I am very low.
Rescue me from my persecutors,
 for they are too strong for me.
⁷Bring me out of prison
 so I can thank you.
The godly will crowd around me,
 for you treat me kindly."

## PSALM 143

*A psalm of David.*

¹Hear my prayer, O LORD;
 listen to my plea!
 Answer me because you are faithful and
  righteous.
²Don't bring your servant to trial!
 Compared to you, no one is perfect.
³My enemy has chased me.
 He has knocked me to the ground.
 He forces me to live in darkness like those
  in the grave.
⁴I am losing all hope;
 I am paralyzed with fear.
⁵I remember the days of old.
 I ponder all your great works.
 I think about what you have done.
⁶I reach out for you.
 I thirst for you as parched land thirsts for
  rain.    *Interlude*

⁷Come quickly, LORD, and answer me,
 for my depression deepens.
Don't turn away from me,
 or I will die.

*The LORD helps the fallen and lifts up those bent beneath their loads*

PSALM 145:14   The Lord is the God of second chances. I wonder if our heart is as big. I made these letters wider than normal to give them a heavy appearance. This is an example of making up one's own letter style in response to the emotion of the text.

⁸Let me hear of your unfailing love to me
  in the morning,
 for I am trusting you.
Show me where to walk,
 for I have come to you in prayer.
⁹Save me from my enemies, LORD;
 I run to you to hide me.
¹⁰Teach me to do your will,
 for you are my God.
May your gracious Spirit lead me forward
 on a firm footing.
¹¹For the glory of your name, O LORD, save me.

In your righteousness, bring me out of this
    distress.
¹²In your unfailing love, cut off all my enemies
    and destroy all my foes,
      for I am your servant.

## PSALM 144
*A psalm of David.*

¹Bless the LORD, who is my rock.
    He gives me strength for war
    and skill for battle.
²He is my loving ally and my fortress,
    my tower of safety, my deliverer.
    He stands before me as a shield, and I take
      refuge in him.
    He subdues the nations* under me.

³O LORD, what are mortals that you should
    notice us,
    mere humans that you should care for us?
⁴For we are like a breath of air;
    our days are like a passing shadow.

⁵Bend down the heavens, LORD, and come
    down.
    Touch the mountains so they billow smoke.
⁶Release your lightning bolts and scatter your
    enemies!
    Release your arrows and confuse them!
⁷Reach down from heaven and rescue me;
    deliver me from deep waters,
    from the power of my enemies.
⁸Their mouths are full of lies;
    they swear to tell the truth, but they lie.

⁹I will sing a new song to you, O God!
    I will sing your praises with a ten-stringed
    harp.
¹⁰For you grant victory to kings!
    You are the one who rescued your servant
    David.
¹¹Save me from the fatal sword!
    Rescue me from the power of my enemies.
    Their mouths are full of lies;
    they swear to tell the truth, but they lie.

¹²May our sons flourish in their youth
    like well-nurtured plants.
    May our daughters be like graceful pillars,
    carved to beautify a palace.
¹³May our farms be filled
    with crops of every kind.
    May the flocks in our fields multiply by the
      thousands,
    even tens of thousands,
¹⁴   and may our oxen be loaded down with
      produce.
    May there be no breached walls, no forced exile,
    no cries of distress in our squares.
¹⁵Yes, happy are those who have it like this!
    Happy indeed are those whose God is the
    LORD.

## PSALM 145
*A psalm of praise of David.*

¹I will praise you, my God and King,
    and bless your name forever and ever.
²I will bless you every day,
    and I will praise you forever.
³Great is the LORD! He is most worthy
    of praise!
    His greatness is beyond discovery!

⁴Let each generation tell its children
    of your mighty acts.
⁵I will meditate* on your majestic, glorious
    splendor
    and your wonderful miracles.
⁶Your awe-inspiring deeds will be on every
    tongue;
    I will proclaim your greatness.
⁷Everyone will share the story of your
    wonderful goodness;
    they will sing with joy of your righteousness.

🖋 PSALM 147:4-5, 16-18   The staggering magnitude of the universe helps us imagine God's greatness. And we begin to understand why he is to be feared. Meteorologists do their best to predict weather, but only God can *make* it. Considering the contrast between the immensity of any single star and the microscopic intricacy of one snowflake puts God in perspective.

---

**144:2** Some manuscripts read *my people.* **145:5** Some manuscripts read *They will speak.*

HE COUNTS THE STARS
AND CALLS THEM ALL BY NAME
HE SENDS THE SNOW LIKE WHITE WOOL
HE SCATTERS FROST UPON THE GROUND
LIKE ASHES

HE HURLS THE HAIL LIKE STONES
WHO CAN STAND AGAINST HIS FREEZING COLD?

THEN
AT HIS COMMAND
IT ALL MELTS
He sends his winds
AND THE ICE THAWS

HOW
GREAT IS
OUR LORD
HIS POWER IS ABSOLUTE

HIS UNDERSTANDING IS BEYOND COMPREHENSION

⁸The LORD is kind and merciful,
  slow to get angry, full of unfailing love.
⁹The LORD is good to everyone.
  He showers compassion on all his creation.
¹⁰All of your works will thank you, LORD,
  and your faithful followers will bless you.
¹¹They will talk together about the glory of your
    kingdom;
  they will celebrate examples of your power.
¹²They will tell about your mighty deeds
  and about the majesty and glory of your
    reign.
¹³For your kingdom is an everlasting kingdom.
  You rule generation after generation.

  The LORD is faithful in all he says;
  he is gracious in all he does.★
¹⁴The LORD helps the fallen
  and lifts up those bent beneath their loads.
¹⁵All eyes look to you for help;
  you give them their food as they need it.
¹⁶When you open your hand,
  you satisfy the hunger and thirst of every
    living thing.

¹⁷The LORD is righteous in everything he does;
  he is filled with kindness.
¹⁸The LORD is close to all who call on him,
  yes, to all who call on him sincerely.
¹⁹He fulfills the desires of those who fear him;
  he hears their cries for help and rescues
    them.
²⁰The LORD protects all those who love him,
  but he destroys the wicked.

²¹I will praise the LORD,
  and everyone on earth will bless his holy
    name
  forever and forever.

## PSALM 146

¹Praise the LORD!

  Praise the LORD, I tell myself.
²I will praise the LORD as long as I live.
  I will sing praises to my God even with my
    dying breath.

³Don't put your confidence in powerful people;
  there is no help for you there.
⁴When their breathing stops, they return to the
    earth,
  and in a moment all their plans come to an
    end.
⁵But happy are those who have the God of
    Israel★ as their helper,
  whose hope is in the LORD their God.
⁶He is the one who made heaven and earth,
  the sea, and everything in them.
  He is the one who keeps every promise
    forever,
⁷  who gives justice to the oppressed
  and food to the hungry.
  The LORD frees the prisoners.
⁸  The LORD opens the eyes of the blind.
  The LORD lifts the burdens of those bent
    beneath their loads.
  The LORD loves the righteous.
⁹The LORD protects the foreigners among us.
  He cares for the orphans and widows,
  but he frustrates the plans of the wicked.

¹⁰The LORD will reign forever.
  O Jerusalem,★ your God is King in every
    generation!

  Praise the LORD!

## PSALM 147

¹Praise the LORD!

  How good it is to sing praises to our God!
  How delightful and how right!
²The LORD is rebuilding Jerusalem
  and bringing the exiles back to Israel.
³He heals the brokenhearted,
  binding up their wounds.
⁴He counts the stars
  and calls them all by name.

🖋 PSALM 148:11-13  It is God's will for all his
creation to praise him. It must give him great
pleasure when we, who have a choice, do so. I am
more at home with calligraphy than with illustration.
This naive style freed me to draw people in all their
diversity.

**145:13** The last two lines of 145:13 are not found in many of the ancient manuscripts.  **146:5** Hebrew *of Jacob.*  **146:10** Hebrew *Zion.*

# KINGS
## OF THE EARTH
AND **all people**
all people all people

# RULERS
AND **JUDGES**
of the earth

**YOUNG MEN**
AND *maidens*
**OLD MEN**
AND children

*Let them all praise the name of the LORD*

5 How great is our Lord! His power is
　　absolute!
　　His understanding is beyond compre-
　　　hension!
6 The LORD supports the humble,
　　but he brings the wicked down into the
　　　dust.

7 Sing out your thanks to the LORD;
　　sing praises to our God, accompanied by
　　　harps.
8 He covers the heavens with clouds,
　　provides rain for the earth,
　　and makes the green grass grow in mountain
　　　pastures.
9 He feeds the wild animals,
　　and the young ravens cry to him for food.
10 The strength of a horse does not impress
　　　him;
　　how puny in his sight is the strength of a
　　　man.
11 Rather, the LORD's delight is in those who
　　　honor him,
　　those who put their hope in his unfailing
　　　love.

12 Praise the LORD, O Jerusalem!
　　Praise your God, O Zion!
13 For he has fortified the bars of your gates
　　and blessed your children within you.
14 He sends peace across your nation
　　and satisfies you with plenty of the finest
　　　wheat.
15 He sends his orders to the world—
　　how swiftly his word flies!
16 He sends the snow like white wool;
　　he scatters frost upon the ground like ashes.
17 He hurls the hail like stones.
　　Who can stand against his freezing cold?
18 Then, at his command, it all melts.
　　He sends his winds, and the ice thaws.

19 He has revealed his words to Jacob,
　　his principles and laws to Israel.
20 He has not done this with any other nation;
　　they do not know his laws.

　　Praise the LORD!

# PSALM 148

1 Praise the LORD!

Praise the LORD from the heavens!
　　Praise him from the skies!
2 Praise him, all his angels!
　　Praise him, all the armies of heaven!
3 Praise him, sun and moon!
　　Praise him, all you twinkling stars!
4 Praise him, skies above!
　　Praise him, vapors high above the
　　　clouds!
5 Let every created thing give praise to the
　　　LORD,
　　for he issued his command, and they
　　　came into being.
6 He established them forever and forever.
　　His orders will never be revoked.

7 Praise the LORD from the earth,
　　you creatures of the ocean depths,
8 fire and hail, snow and storm,
　　wind and weather that obey him,
9 mountains and all hills,
　　fruit trees and all cedars,
10 wild animals and all livestock,
　　reptiles and birds,
11 kings of the earth and all people,
　　rulers and judges of the earth,
12 young men and maidens,
　　old men and children.
13 Let them all praise the name of the LORD.
　　For his name is very great;
　　his glory towers over the earth and
　　　heaven!
14 He has made his people strong,
　　honoring his godly ones—
　　the people of Israel who are close to him.

　　Praise the LORD!

✒ PSALM 150:3-6   This is the grand finale, and it is
loud!  Blasting trumpets, clashing cymbals, and dancing
are endorsed, and yet there is room for the small voice
of the flute. The repetition of "Praise him" is an anchor-
ing contrast to all the different sounds being expressed.
All is directed toward the one who is worthy of our
praise. Hallelujah!

PRAISE HIM
with a blast of the trumpet
PRAISE HIM
With the lyre and harp
PRAISE HIM
WITH THE TAMBOURINE
and
dancing
PRAISE HIM
with
stringed instruments
and flutes
PRAISE HIM
with a clash of cymbals
PRAISE HIM
with loud clanging cymbals
LET EVERYTHING THAT LIVES
sing praises
TO
THE LORD

## PSALM 149

¹Praise the LORD!

Sing to the LORD a new song.
  Sing his praises in the assembly of the
    faithful.
²O Israel, rejoice in your Maker.
  O people of Jerusalem,* exult in your
    King.
³Praise his name with dancing,
  accompanied by tambourine and harp.
⁴For the LORD delights in his people;
  he crowns the humble with salvation.
⁵Let the faithful rejoice in this honor.
  Let them sing for joy as they lie on their
    beds.
⁶Let the praises of God be in their mouths,
  and a sharp sword in their hands—
⁷to execute vengeance on the nations
  and punishment on the peoples,
⁸to bind their kings with shackles
  and their leaders with iron chains,

**149:2** Hebrew *Zion.*

⁹to execute the judgment written against them.
  This is the glory of his faithful ones.

Praise the LORD!

## PSALM 150

¹Praise the LORD!

Praise God in his heavenly dwelling;
  praise him in his mighty heaven!
²Praise him for his mighty works;
  praise his unequaled greatness!
³Praise him with a blast of the trumpet;
  praise him with the lyre and harp!
⁴Praise him with the tambourine and dancing;
  praise him with stringed instruments and
    flutes!
⁵Praise him with a clash of cymbals;
  praise him with loud clanging cymbals.
⁶Let everything that lives sing praises to the
    LORD!

Praise the LORD!

The text was set in Bembo
and was composed by Gwen Elliott
at Tyndale House.
The text paper is 70 pound
New Life Opaque Vellum,
the spine material is Devon cloth,
the cover material is Permalin,
and the end papers are
Rainbow Antique.